Popular Reading for Children IV

A Collection of *Booklist* Columns

Edited by Sally Estes

BOOKLIST Publications
American Library Association
1999

ISBN 0-8389-8010-4

Table of Contents

Introduction

This fourth book in a series of compilations of retrospective popular-reading lists for children features a tantalizing mix of genres and subjects, ranging from ribtickling fractured fairy tales, fantasies, scary tales, and mysteries to poetry, religion, art books, and the winning of the West. In short, there is something here that will appeal to a wide variety of reading tastes and ability. Books to be read to the young are also included.

As always, emphasis is on the appeal to children as well as the quality of the books included. Some of the 15 bibliographies have been updated from their original publication in *Booklist*; others have been created especially for this book.

A special thanks goes to Michelle Rosenthal, librarian at the James Russell Lowell School in Chicago, Illinois, for bibliographic help and for her many kid-tested suggestions for the lists.

Sally Estes
Editor, Books for Youth
Booklist

Turning the Tail on Fairy Tales

by Sally Estes

Fractured fairy tales have come a long way over the years. Some recent titles have extra bite, which often gives the story a darker edge and a more sophisticated sensibility, even in some of the picture-book versions. Listed below are titles published in the 1990s that will provoke thought or laughter or both.

Fiction

Brooke, William J. Untold Tales. 1992. HarperCollins, lib. ed., $14.89 (0-06-020272-6).

Gr. 5–9. In this group of stories gone awry, the princess pouts because she likes her husband as he was—green and croaking; Beauty is hideous, and it's the Beast whose looks are perfect; Prince Charming arrives 25 years too late to kiss his Sleeping Beauty, having married Cinderella on the way.

Conford, Ellen. The Frog Princess of Pelham. 1997. Little, Brown, $15.95 (0-316-15246-3).

Gr. 5–7. Chandler, a wealthy orphan, is kissed by Danny, the school's prince of popularity, and turns into a frog.

Levine, Gail Carson. Ella Enchanted. 1997. HarperCollins, $14.95 (0-06-027510-3).

Gr. 5–8. In this enchanting retelling of the Cinderella story, Ella is blessed by a fairy at birth with the gift of obedience, but to her horror, Ella must literally do what everyone tells her, from sweeping the floor to giving up a beloved heirloom necklace.

Napoli, Donna J. The Prince of the Pond: Otherwise Known as De Fawg Pin. 1992. illus. Dutton, lib. ed., $14.99 (0-525-44976-0); Penguin/Puffin, paper, $4.99 (0-14-037151-6).

Gr. 3–6. In this takeoff on the frog-prince motif, the story is told from the point of view of Jade, a female frog who meets the prince when he first becomes a frog but never quite catches on to the fact that he's more than just a frog—even as she teaches him the ropes of being one. The sequel is *Jimmy, the Pickpocket of the Palace* (1995).

Picture Books

Ada, Alma Flore. Yours Truly, Goldilocks. Illus. by Leslie Tryon. 1998. Simon & Schuster/Atheneum, $16 (0-689-81608-1).

Ages 4–7. In this sequel to *Dear Peter Rabbit* (1994), a housewarming party is planned for the Three Little Pigs through a series of letters between the pigs, Goldilocks, Baby Bear, and Little Red Riding Hood, but big, bad cousins Wolfy Lupus and Fer O'Cious are making plans that spell trouble for the party-goers.

Buehner, Caralyn. Fanny's Dream. Illus. by Mark Buehner. 1996. Dial, $14.99 (0-8037-1496-3).

Ages 6–9. The Cinderella story is retold with a twist in this ebullient mix of storytelling and art from a husband-and-wife team with a fine sense of humor.

Edwards, Pamela Duncan. Dinorella: A Prehistoric Fairytale. Illus. by Henry Cole. 1997. Hyperion; dist. by Little, Brown, $15.95 (0-7868-0309-6).

Ages 5–8. Her fairy godmother, Fairy-dactyl, has prettied her up with diamonds, but Dinorella isn't content to wait around like the classic fairy-tale gal; instead, she saves the day by dumbfounding the dreaded *Deinonychus*, who is determined to make Duke Dudley his dinner.

Egielski, Richard. The Gingerbread Boy. 1997. illus. HarperCollins/Laura Geringer, $14.95 (0-06-026030-0).

Ages 2–6. The popular tale is transported with wild farce from its traditional barnyard setting to the crowded streets of New York City today as the escaping gingerbread boy is chased down the fire escape, past garbage cans, across wash lines, into the subway, through the park . . .

Emberley, Michael. Ruby. 1990. illus. Little, Brown, paper, $5.95 (0-316-23660-8).

Ages 4–6. Transplanting "Little Red Riding Hood" from the country to the streets of Boston, Emberley portrays Ruby, a no-nonsense mouse, who treks across town to deliver her ailing granny some freshly baked pies, dodging all sorts of danger and outwitting the cat who plans on eating Grandmother as an appetizer and Ruby as the main course.

Ernst, Lisa Campbell. Little Red Riding Hood: A Newfangled Prairie Tale. 1995. illus. Simon & Schuster, $15 (0-689-80145-9).

Ages 5–8. This Red Riding Hood wears a hooded sweatshirt as she pedals across the prairie to Grandma's, and when the wolf appears, it's not Grandma he wants but her secret recipe for muffins. Gloriously goofy oversize art makes this great for primary-grade story hours.

Harris, Jim. Jack and the Giant: A Story Full of Beans. 1997. illus. Northland/Rising Moon, $15.95 (0-87358-680-8).

Ages 5–9. In a pun-filled tale that gives the classic "Jack and the Beanstalk" a southwestern twist, Jack and his mother, Annie Okey-Dokey, live on a ranch in Arizona, and the magic beanstalk this time leads to an adobe castle in the sky, where Jack encounters the giant cattle-rustler Wild Bill Hiccup—all caught in the big, bright cartoon-style art.

Jackson, Ellen. Cinder Edna. Illus. by Kevin O'Malley. 1994. Lothrop, $16 (0-688-12322-8).

Ages 4–8. The traditional passive Cinderella is the neighbor of liberated Cinder Edna, and where Cinderella needs a fairy godmother to get her to the ball, Cinder Edna earns the money mowing lawns and cleaning parrot cages, and she takes the bus to the ball, where she attracts the attention of the boring prince's younger brother, who looks a lot like Woody Allen.

Kellogg, Steven. The Three Little Pigs. 1997. illus. Morrow, $16 (0-688-08731-0).

Ages 5–8. When Serafina Sow turns her traveling waffle business over to her three children, the traditional tale takes off at high speed, with some entirely new details, which include Tempesto the wicked wolf getting his comeuppance in a pyrotechnic finish.

Ketteman, Helen. Bubba, the Cowboy Prince: A Fractured Texas Tale. Illus. by James Warhola. 1997. Scholastic, $15.95 (0-590-25506-1).

Ages 5–8. In this western version of

3

the Cinderella story, the fairy godmother is a cow, the Cinderella role is played by a likable Texas cowboy named Bubba, and the handsome prince's part is taken by Miz Lurleen, a spunky (and wealthy) cowgirl.

Lowell, Susan. Little Red Cowboy Hat. Illus. by Randy Cecil. 1997. Holt, $14.95 (0-8050-3508-7).

Ages 5–8. Little Red Riding Hood gets a Wild West twist in a funny version that sticks pretty close to the plot but has a tall-tale twang in the telling. Lowell teams up with illustrator Tom Curry for *The Bootmaker and the Elves* (1997), which sticks closely to the original plot but is set in the Old West and stars a poor cowboy bootmaker.

McNaughton, Colin. Oops! 1997. illus. Harcourt, lib. ed., $14 (0-15-201588-4).

Ages 3–6. After getting nowhere in *Suddenly* (1995), the big, bad wolf is back for another try at Preston Pig, and the simple-hearted Preston, this time decked out in Little Red Riding Hood garb, leads the toothy villain on a merry chase right to Grandma's house.

Meddaugh, Susan. Cinderella's Rat. 1997. illus. Houghton, $15 (0-395-86833-5).

Ages 5–7. Everyone knows what happened to Cinderella at midnight, but what about the rat who was changed into a coachman?

Minters, Frances. Sleepless Beauty. Illus. by G. Brian Karas. 1996. Viking, $14.99 (0-670-87033-1).

Ages 5–8. Beauty narrates her story to a hip-hop beat: "The day I was born / I was such a cutie / Mom and Dad called me / Their own Little Beauty," and Karas portrays all the action in a present-day New York City setting, with the witch pricking Beauty's finger on a phonograph needle. Minters and Karas also pair up for a rollicking *Cinder-Elly* (1994).

Nikola-Lisa, W. Shake Dem Halloween Bones. Illus. by Mike Reed. 1997. Houghton, $16 (0-395-73095-3).

Ages 3–7. In this rhythmic, joyful picture book, cool, contemporary Cinderella, Rapunzel, Tom Thumb, and other storybook creatures in sneakers and shades "shake shake dem bones" and party, party, party.

Quindlen, Anna. Happily Ever After. Illus. by James Stevenson. 1997. Viking, $13.99 (0-670-86961-9).

Gr. 2–4, younger for reading aloud. When a magic baseball mitt transforms fourth-grader Kate into a princess in a medieval castle, the tomboy eschews mandatory ladylike pursuits to help slay a dragon, teach a witch and a troll to play games, and set up a baseball game between the maids and the ladies-in-waiting. Stevenson's illustrations combine the laid-back, the silly, and the wild.

Scieszka, Jon. The Stinky Cheese Man and Other Fairly Stupid Tales. Illus. by Lane Smith. 1992. Viking, $16.99 (0-670-84487-X); paper, $5.99 (0-14-055878-0).

Gr. 2 and up. In a book bursting with wry wit, wordplay, and wacky jokes, Scieszka and Smith turn a host of fairy tales upside down and recast them with art that captures the comic tellings. Don't miss the wacky pair's *The True Story of the Three Little Pigs! by A Wolf* (1989) or Scieszka's *The Frog Prince, Continued* (1991), illustrated by Steve Johnson.

Stanley, Diane. Rumpelstiltskin's Daughter. 1997. illus. Morrow, $15 (0-688-14327-X).

Ages 5–9. This witty mix of fable and farce features a king who's as stupid as he is greedy and a sly 16-year-old damsel, daughter of Rumpelstiltskin and the miller's daughter, who, like her mother, is captured and ordered to spin straw into gold, and who also turns the tables on the king.

Trivizas, Eugene. The Three Little Wolves and the Big Bad Pig. Illus. by Helen Oxenbury. 1993. Simon & Schuster/Margaret K. McElderry, lib. ed., $17 (0-689-50569-8); paper, $5.99 (0-689-81528-X).

Ages 5–9. This fractured fairy tale with its subtle message that beauty can facilitate change and that tenderness works better than toughness also fea-tures art and text that are filled with wit.

Vozar, David. Rapunzel: A Happenin' Rap. Illus. by Betsy Lewin. 1998. Doubleday, $15.95 (0-385-32314-X).

Ages 4–7. Like Vozar and Lewin's *M. C. Turtle and the Hip Hop Hare* (1996), this happenin' rap gives an old story an urban setting, a rhythmic beat, and a contemporary silliness that's picked up in the wild, scribbled cartoons with thick lines and neon colors.

Tripping the Book Fantastic

by Sally Estes

Fantasies have long been favorites of children, whether they are the Oz books or the Narnia series or today's Redwall saga. The following bibliography lists some of the best fantasies published for children in the 1990s.

Avi. City of Light, City of Dark: A Comic-Book Novel. Illus. by Brian Floca. 1993. Orchard/Richard Jackson, paper, $7.95 (0-531-07058-1).

Gr. 6–9. This graphic novel is about Sarah Stubbs, about her father's secret, and about saving Manhattan from the Kurbs, the creatures that really own the island.

Barron, T. A. The Lost Years of Merlin. 1996. Putnam/Philomel, $19.95 (0-399-23018-1).

Gr. 7–10. In the first volume of a five-book series about Merlin, the amnesiac youth embarks on a quest to the mysterious isle of Fincayra ("not of the Earth, nor of the Otherworld") in search of his true name and heritage. The sequels so far are *The Seven Songs of Merlin* (1997) and *The Fires of Merlin* (1998). Barron is also the author of the fantasy trilogy: *Heartlight* (1990), *The Ancient One* (1992), and *The Merlin Effect* (1994).

Bell, Clare. Ratha's Challenge. 1994. Macmillan/Margaret K. McElderry, $16.95 (0-689-50586-8).

Gr. 6–12. The latest episode in Bell's series about the Named clan of prehistoric cats has the Named confronting a strange clan of hunter cats that is driven by and completely dependent upon the telepathic song of its leader. The saga begins with *Ratha's Creature* (1982).

The Book of Dragons. Ed. and illus. by Michael Hague. 1995. Morrow, $18 (0-688-10879-2).

Gr. 4–7. These 17 classic dragon tales, illustrated in Hague's bold signature style, will whet the appetites of the dragon-lovers among us.

Cooper, Susan. The Boggart. 1993. Macmillan/Margaret K. McElderry, $14.95 (0-689-50576-0); paper, $3.95 (0-689-80173-4).

Gr. 4–6. A centuries-old Scottish spirit, endearing and maddening in the same breath, wreaks havoc on a modern-day family. The sequel is *The Boggart and the Monster* (1997).

Coville, Bruce. Into the Land of the Unicorns. 1994. Scholastic, $13.95 (0-590-45955-4); paper, $3.50 (0-590-45956-2).

Gr. 4–6. Eleven-year-old Cara narrowly escapes being captured on Earth by "leaping" to Luster, the land of the unicorns, only to find that she is being pursued there as well. Also by Coville, *Goblins in the Castle* (1992).

Friesner, Esther M. Wishing Season. Illus. by Frank Kelly Freas. 1993. Simon & Schuster/Atheneum, $14.95 (0-689-31574-0).

Gr. 7–10. In this zany tale, arrogant Khalid, the best student in genie school, gets in deep trouble when he's allowed to go into a lamp for a trial run and inadvertently gives a stray cat three wishes.

Hite, Sid. Answer My Prayer. 1995. Holt, $15.95 (0-8050-3406-4); Dell, paper, $3.99 (0-440-22014-9).

Gr. 7–10. Hite blends the ordinary with the exciting and then adds a dollop of the miraculous when Lydia meets, first, a fortune-teller and then a quirky sleepyhead of an angel who champions her dreams—between naps.

Jacques, Brian. The Pearls of Lutra. 1997. Putnam/Philomel, $19.95 (0-399-22946-9).

Gr. 5–8. The ninth novel in the rich Redwall saga, an ongoing animal fantasy that features no magic, continues the face-off between the good beasts of Redwall Abbey and evil forces consisting of "corsairs, searats, and all manner of vermin wavescum."

Kindl, Patrice. Owl in Love. 1993. Houghton, $13.96 (0-395-66162-5); Penguin/Puffin, $3.99 (0-14-037129-X).

Gr. 5–9. Fourteen-year-old Owl Tycho, who can transform from human to owl at will, senses a connection between a starving, wild-eyed boy and an inept owl, whom she literally takes under her wing and feeds the prey she catches.

King-Smith, Dick. Three Terrible Trins. Illus. by Mark Teague. 1994. Crown, $15 (0-517-59828-0).

Gr. 3–5. A deftly written, fast-paced animal fantasy starring three young mice who are determined to avenge their father's death by making life miserable for the household cats.

Levy, Robert. Clan of the Shape-Changers. 1994. Houghton, $13.95 (0-395-66612-0).

Gr. 6–9. When the evil shaman is questioning all green-eyed inhabitants of Reune, supposedly to rid the country of witches, green-eyed 16-year-old Susan must leave her village with her wolf, Farrun, because she is a shape-changer. Levy is also the author of *Escape from Exile* (1993).

McGraw, Eloise. The Moorchild. 1996. Simon & Schuster/Margaret K. McElderry, $16 (0-689-80654-X).

Gr. 4–6. Half-fairy and half-human, Moql grew up with the fairy folk until, feeling that she might be a danger to the folk, they changed her into a baby and switched her with a human infant; she grows up again, a changeling who struggles with her nature, her memories, and the ties that bind her to both worlds.

McKinley, Robin. Rose Daughter. 1997. Greenwillow, $16 (0-688-15439-5).

Gr. 6–12. Almost 20 years after *Beauty* (1975), McKinley returns to the Beauty and the Beast fairy tale, creating an even richer, more mystical, and darker story, though leavened with humor, of the merchant's youngest daughter, who goes to live in the Beast's castle to save her father.

Nix, Garth. Sabriel. 1996. HarperCollins, $15.95 (0-06-027322-4).

Gr. 7–12. A complex and enthralling fantasy in which Sabriel, daughter of the mage Abhorsen, must enter the Old Kingdom and the realm of Death in search of her missing father.

Pierce, Tamora. The Realms of the Gods. 1996. Simon & Schuster/Atheneum, $17 (0-689-31990-8).

Gr. 6–10. In the fourth and final book in The Immortals fantasy series, Daine and the mage Numair face off against the evil Stormwing and the Queen of Chaos, with the help of the dragons, other immortals, and, in the end, the gods themselves. Previous adventures are *Wild Magic* (1992), *Wolf-Speaker* (1994), and *Emperor Mage* (1995).

Pullman, Phillip. The Golden Compass. 1996. Knopf, $20 (0-679-87924-2); Ballantine/Del Rey, paper, $5.99 (0-345-41335-0).

Gr. 6–12. A resilient young hero named Lyra, an amulet that can answer questions, companion daemons, kidnapped children, formidable armored bears, witch clans, and more are featured in this high-adventure high fantasy. Book 2 of His Dark Materials is *The Subtle Knife* (1997).

Sherman, Josepha. Gleaming Bright. 1994. Walker, $16.95 (0-8027-8296-5).

Gr. 5–8. This fast-paced fantasy features a princess who flees an arranged marriage and goes in search of a magical box named Gleaming Bright, which she can use to save her kingdom.

Smith, Sherwood. Crown Duel. 1997. Harcourt/Jane Yolen, $17 (0-15-201608-2).

Gr. 5–8. In this tale of daring adventure, intrigue, and honor, young Meliara and her brother, Bran, promise their dying father that they will rise against wicked King Galdran and protect their lands and the Covenant, an age-old promise to the mysterious Hill People. Book 1 of the Crown and Court Duet. An earlier sword-and-sorcery trilogy consists of *Wren to the Rescue* (1990), *Wren's Quest* (1993), and *Wren's War* (1995).

Sonenklar, Carol. Bug Boy. 1997. illus. Holt, $14.95 (0-8050-4794-8).

Gr. 3–6. When someone sends Charlie, known to his friends as Bug Boy because of his appreciation for bugs, a Bug-a-View, which mysteriously promises a bug's-eye view of the world, Charlie finds life very adventurous as he turns into a variety of bugs.

Sterman, Betsy and **Sterman, Samuel.** Backyard Dragon. 1993. illus. Harper-Collins, $14 (0-06-020783-3).

Gr. 3–5. Wyrdryn, a fifteenth-century Welsh dragon, is banished by the wizard Gwilym to Kings Ridge, New Jersey, and the twentieth century, where young Owen discovers the beast; however, no one else believes in the dragon's existence.

Turner, Megan Whalen. The Thief. 1996. Greenwillow, $15 (0-688-14627-9).

Gr. 5–8. If Gen, a gifted young thief imprisoned for life, can steal for the king's magus a legendary stone hidden in a mysterious temple, the magus will set him free.

Winthrop, Elizabeth. The Battle for the Castle. 1993. Holiday, $14.95 (0-8234-1010-2).

Gr. 4–7. In a sequel to *The Castle in the Attic* (1985), William receives a magic token for his birthday, along with a note about love, courage, and loyalty—and a reminder that, now 12, he can become a squire; entering the castle again, William and his friend Jason find themselves caught up in a wild drama involving an ancient chant foretelling the return of evil.

Wrede, Patricia C. Talking to Dragons. 1993. Harcourt, $16.95 (0-15-284247-0); Scholastic, paper, $4.50 (0-590-48475-3).

Gr. 6–10. In the fourth entry in the Enchanted Forest Chronicles, Cimorene's son, Daystar, now 16, embarks on a mystifying grand adventure during which a hotheaded fire witch and a very young dragon in search of its own princess join Daystar in rescuing his father, King Mendanbar. The previous diverting books are *Dealing with Dragons* (1990), *Searching for Dragons* (1991), and *Calling on Dragons* (1993).

Yarbro, Chelsea Quinn. Monet's Ghost. 1997. illus. Simon & Schuster/Atheneum, $17 (0-689-80732-5).

Gr. 6–10. Geena Howe, 15, has the

ability to think herself into a painting, and when she enters a huge Monet, she finds herself in a bizarre place where stacks of wheat, moats, and castle towers appear and disappear after the appearance of a ghostly figure.

Yolen, Jane. Merlin. 1997. Harcourt, $15 (0-15-200814-4).

Gr. 5–8. The concluding volume in the Young Merlin trilogy finds Hawk-Hobby, whose true name is Merlin, escaping from a village of wild folk with the help of a small child named Cub, who happens to be the once and future King Arthur. The first two books are *Passager* (1996) and *Hobby* (1996).

Zambreno, Mary Frances. Journeyman Wizard. 1994. Harcourt, $16.95 (0-15-200022-4); Hyperion; dist. by Little, Brown, paper, $5.95 (0-7868-1127-7).

Gr. 4–7. In the sequel to *A Plague of Sorcerers* (1991), student wizard Jermyn Graves is apprehensive but excited to be studying with the formidable master spell-maker but finds himself accused of murder when a freak accident causes a death in the household.

Folktale Favorites

by the Books for Youth Staff

The Books for Youth editors have chosen their own favorite folktales and fairy tales—the versions that have stuck with them over the years. This list is not intended to be inclusive; it is strictly personal, but one that might introduce you to some new stories or remind you of your own favorites. What fun!

Aardema, Verna. Why Mosquitoes Buzz in People's Ears. Illus. by Leo Dillon and Diane Dillon. 1975. Dial, $15.99 (0-8037-6087-6); paper, $4.95 (0-8037-6089-2).

Ages 5–7. The Dillons' cut shapes of varying hues assembled into stylized scenes create a polished, dramatic visual panorama that is well matched by Aardema's onomatopoeic text relating how a mosquito's silly lie to an iguana sets in motion a cumulative series of events.

Andersen, Hans Christian. The Snow Queen. Adapt. by Amy Erlich. Illus. by Susan Jeffers. 1982. Dial, lib. ed., $12.89 (0-8037-8029-X); paper, $4.95 (0-8037-0692-8).

Gr. 3–4. A pared-down version of the original story, this combines a smoothly moving text with absorbing art. Jeffers' riveting double-page spreads make excellent use of her crosshatching skills.

Bernier-Grand, Carmen T. Juan Bobo: Four Folktales from Puerto Rico. Illus. by Ernesto Ramos Nieves. 1994. HarperCollins, $14 (0-06-023389-3).

Gr. 1–3. True to their oral tradition, these comic tales about Juan Bobo, a classic fool character, are told with immediacy and spirit and illustrated with exuberant folk-style illustrations in bright tropical colors. Part of the I Can Read series, this can also be used with younger children as a read-aloud.

Brown, Marcia. Stone Soup. 1991 (orig. pub. 1947). illus. Simon & Schuster, $14.95 (0-684-92296-7); paper, $5.99 (0-689-71103-4).

Ages 4–8. Brown's version of the old tale about the soldiers who trick villagers who had denied them food into providing all the ingredients—except the stones—for soup fit for a king is simply told and illustrated with colorful action pictures that carry the story's flavor and underlying humor.

Bruchac, Joseph. The Boy Who Lived with the Bears and Other Iroquois Stories. 1995. illus. HarperCollins, $15.95 (0-06-021287-X).

Gr. 4–6. Direct, immediate language makes this collection of Iroquois teaching tales just right for a wide audience, and the humor inherent in the stories makes them perfect for reading and telling aloud.

Cooper, Susan. The Silver Cow. Illus. by Warwick Hutton. 1983. Simon & Schuster/Margaret K. McElderry, $15 (0-689-50236-2); paper, $4.95 (0-689-71512-9).

Gr. 1–3. Words and artwork are balanced between the concrete and the mystical in this Welsh story of a greedy farmer who reaps the rewards of his son's forbidden harp-playing in the form of a silver cow. Hutton's contrast of light and shadow seems to magnetize the colors, giving drama to both the indoor and outdoor scenes.

Galdone, Joanna. The Tailypo: A Ghost Story. Illus. by Paul Galdone. 1977. Clarion, paper, $6.95 (0-395-30084-3).

Ages 5–7. "Tailypo, tailypo, all I want is my tailypo." The telling is smooth and the illustrations rich in this tale of an old man and his three dogs, who prove no match for the single-minded creature that wants its tail back after the old man chops it off and eats it.

Goble, Paul. Buffalo Woman. 1984. illus. Simon & Schuster/Bradbury, $14.95 (0-02-737720-2); paper, $4.95 (0-689-71109-3).

Ages 5–9. This myth commemorating the kinship of the Great Plains Indians with the buffalo features Goble's signature stylized artwork in vibrant colors. It handsomely portrays the harmony between humans, animals, and other manifestations of nature.

Haley, Gail E. Jack and the Bean Tree. 1986. illus. Crown, $13.95 (0-517-55717-7).

Ages 5–8. An Appalachian variant of *Jack and the Beanstalk* contains language that is folksy and nicely cadenced as well as distinctive woodcuts that work well with the homespun text. Good storytellin'.

Hamilton, Virginia. The People Could Fly: American Black Folk Tales. Illus. by Leo Dillon and Diane Dillon. 1985. Knopf, paper, $13 (0-679-85465-7).

Gr. 4–9. A representative collection of 24 black folktales, dramatically retold with spirit and poetry and illustrated by the Dillons with vigor and beauty.

Kellogg, Steven. Paul Bunyan: A Tall Tale. 1984. illus. Morrow, $16 (0-688-03849-2); paper, $5.95 (0-688-05800-0).

Ages 5–9. With clever, extravagantly detailed pictures and an effervescent text, this splendid retelling of the life of the legendary American woodsman deserves its place as one of children's favorites.

Lee, Jeanne M. The Song of Mu Lan. 1995. illus. Front Street, $15.95 (1-886910-00-6).

Gr. 5–9, younger for reading aloud. Disguised as a boy, Mu Lan takes her father's place in the military, proving a formidable soldier during her 12-year service and shocking her fellow soldiers when she appears in womanly garb on her return home. This ancient Chinese folk poem, translated in pleasingly crisp and staccato language, is illustrated with traditionally hued and composed pencil illustrations.

Lester, Julius. The Tales of Uncle Remus: The Adventures of Brer Rabbit. Illus. by Jerry Pinkney. 1987. Dial, $18.99 (0-8037-0271-X).

Gr. 4–9. In the first of several equally fine volumes, Lester ressurects earthy, humorous, vibrant stories drawn from African American tradition in a nearly perfect combination of traditional and modern vernacular that makes them wonderful for reading aloud or storytelling.

McDermott, Gerald. Raven: A Trickster Tale from the Pacific Northwest. 1993. illus. Harcourt, $15 (0-15-265661-8).

Ages 5–9. Handsome, brightly colored artwork inspired by Native Americans of the Pacific Northwest decorates the pages of this delightful, rhythmic tale of the trickster Raven, who steals the sun from the sky people and flings it into the sky to shed light on all.

Paterson, Katherine. The Tale of the Mandarin Ducks. Illus. by Leo Dillon and Diane Dillon. 1990. Dutton/Lodestar, o.p.; Penguin/Puffin Unicorn, paper, $5.99 (0-14-055739-3).

Ages 5–9. In a quiet, dignified retelling of a Japanese fairy tale, a serving girl saves a Mandarin duck from captivity and is rewarded for her efforts. The warm, expressive artwork, which resembles Japanese prints, is a perfect complement.

Perrault, Charles. Puss in Boots. Illus. by Fred Marcellino. 1990. Farrar, $16 (0-374-36160-6).

Ages 5–9. The familiar tale gets a handsome new treatment in this over-size edition. The clever telling and striking art make this a most memorable version.

San Souci, Robert D. Sukey and the Mermaid. Illus. by Brian Pinkney. 1992. Simon & Schuster/Four Winds, $15 (0-02-778141-0); paper, $5.99 (0-689-80718-X).

Ages 5–8. Scratchboard illustrations colored in bold oil pastels add depth and strength to this romantic African American folktale in which a powerful mermaid saves a poor, unhappy girl.

Sanderson, Ruth. Papa Gatto: An Italian Fairy Tale. 1995. illus. Little, Brown, $15.95 (0-316-77073-6).

Gr. 4–6. Lavish, lushly textured artwork combines with elegant, richly descriptive language in this retelling of an unusual Italian tale about a wise cat who sorts out romantic confusion among humans.

Schwartz, Alvin. Scary Stories to Tell in the Dark. Illus. by Stephen Gammell. 1981. HarperCollins/Lippincott, $14.95 (0-397-31926-6).

Gr. 5–7. This collection of stories about witches and ghosts includes "jump" stories as well as macabre songs, contemporary psychic tales, and frightening legends from the past. Gammell's smudge drawings expand the ghoulish atmosphere.

Singer, Isaac Bashevis. When Shlemiel Went to Warsaw and Other Stories. Illus. by Margot Zemach. 1968. Farrar, $13.95 (0-374-38316-2); paper, $4.95 (0-374-48365-5).

Gr. 4–6. From a rich heritage of Yiddish tradition, Singer retells shtetl stories of fools, numskulls, and tricksters. Zemach's pictures capture the humorous characterizations of ordinary people.

Stanley, Diane. Petrosinella: A Neapolitan Rapunzel. 1995. illus. Dial, $14.99 (0-8037-1712-1); NAL, paper, $5.99 (0-14-055491-2).

Ages 4–7. Beautifully designed and handsomely illustrated, this Mediterranean version of Rapunzel introduces a spunkier heroine and adds interesting detail while keeping the flavor of the familiar tale.

Steptoe, John. Mufaro's Beautiful Daughters: An African Tale. 1987. illus. Lothrop, $16 (0-688-04045-4).

Ages 4–7. The universal theme of the good and bad siblings is at the center of this story based on an old African folktale from the area that is now Zimbabwe. The romantic paintings show a lush landscape and a splendid stone city as well as close-up portraits filled with drama and character.

Stevens, Janet. Tops and Bottoms. 1995. illus. Harcourt, $15 (0-15-292851-0).

Ages 4–7. Large, dynamic double-page-spread paintings are only part of the charm of this very funny picture book in which contemporary cousins of Brer Rabbit and Brer Bear begin a business partnership.

Yep, Laurence. The Shell Woman & the King: A Chinese Folktale. Illus. by Yang Ming-Yi. 1993. Dial, $13.99 (0-8037-1394-0).

Ages 5–8. A woman as strong as she

is beautiful is the hero of this Chinese folktale of transformation. The greedy king sets her three increasingly difficult tasks, but she defeats him in the end by transforming his wish into a curse. Yep retells the story in a direct, contemporary style, and the ink-and-watercolor paintings are like scenes under water or in the moonlit sky.

Young, Ed. Lon Po Po: A Red-Riding-Hood Story from China. 1989. illus. Putnam/Philomel, $15.95 (0-399-21619-7); paper, $5.95 (0-698-11382-9).

Ages 6–9. Young incorporates a wolf image into every illustration in this Chinese version of the familiar Red Riding Hood tale, imparting a sense of courage as well as danger.

13

Groundbreakers: 25 Books That Span the Decades

by the Books for Youth Staff

When the Books for Youth staff decided to prepare a bibliography for the special ninetieth anniversary issue of *Booklist*, there was much discussion. Should it contain the best books? The most enduring? The most notable for each decade of *Booklist's* history? Finally, we decided it should be a bibliography of trailblazers, titles that had taken the world of children's publishing in new directions. This decision led to more discussion, as we chose, discarded, and then chose again. What follows is a list of 25 groundbreakers, not necessarily the best or the best loved, but books that changed the face of children's literature forever.

Blume, Judy. Are You There, God? It's Me, Margaret. 1970. Bradbury, o.p.; Dell/Yearling, paper, $3.99 (0-440-90419-6).

God and menstruation were two topics mainstream children's books neatly sidestepped until Blume boldly mixed them in this now-classic book. A forerunner of many first-person stories centered on kids' personal concerns.

Cleary, Beverly. Ramona the Pest. 1968. Morrow, $13.95 (0-688-21721-4); Avon, paper, $4.50 (0-380-70954-6).

Ramona is an American original, certainly among a select handful of characters that almost every young reader knows. Cleary has a sure touch—she mixes the fun of childhood with its more serious moments—and she's been setting a standard for contemporary fiction writers for more than 40 years.

Cormier, Robert. The Chocolate War. 1974. Pantheon, $20 (0-394-82805-4); Dell/Laurel Leaf, paper, $4.50 (0-440-94459-7).

The Chocolate War broke new ground in realistic YA fiction by delivering a strong message about conformity and human manipulation that ends in bleakness, something heretofore considered taboo in YA novels.

Daly, Maureen. Seventeenth Summer. 1947. Archway, paper, $3.50 (0-671-61931-4).

This is the quintessential YA romance, published originally as an adult book before there were any YA romances and retaining its appeal to young romantics through the years.

Fitzhugh, Louise. Harriet the Spy. 1964. HarperCollins, $15.95 (0-06-021910-6); paper, $4.50 (0-06-447165-9).

When *Harriet the Spy* was first published, adults didn't believe children would want to read about a disagreeable young girl who spies on friends and relatives. Today, Harriet is acknowledged as a watershed heroine; her concerns and conflicts have stood the test of time.

Frank, Anne. Anne Frank: The Diary of a Young Girl. Tr. by R. M. Mooyaart. 1958. Many editions available.

The very ordinariness of Anne's daily

concerns while she is hiding in the attic personalizes the sorrow of the Holocaust experience, and her diary initiated a flood of stories about the Nazi nightmare.

Fritz, Jean. And Then What Happened, Paul Revere? Illus. by Margot Tomes. 1973. Putnam, $14.95 (0-698-20274-0); paper, $7.95 (0-698-20541-3).

Fritz was a trailblazer in creating lively, nonfictionalized historical biography featuring dramatic fact to hold children's interest rather than made-up scenes with invented dialogue.

Hamilton, Virginia. Zeely. 1967. illus. Simon & Schuster, $16 (0-02-742470-7); paper, $3.95 (0-689-71695-8).

With *Zeely* in 1967 and *The House of Dies Drear* in 1968, Hamilton opened up the previously all-white world of children's fiction with lyrical, realistic stories of racial identity.

Hinton, S. E. The Outsiders. 1967. Viking, $14.95 (0-670-53257-6); paper, $4.99 (0-14-038572-X).

One of the first YA books about gangs, *The Outsiders* is a candid story that takes teenagers out of a safe, middle-class suburban setting and shows the desperation of needing to belong.

Holland, Isabelle. The Man without a Face. 1972. HarperCollins/Lippincott, o.p.; paper, $4.50 (0-06-447028-8).

One of the first novels to deal with homosexuality, this is a sensitive account of a boy's need for friendship, written with an understanding of the complex issues involved in the search for identity.

Keats, Ezra Jack. The Snowy Day. 1962. Viking, paper, $6.99 (0-670-86733-0).

Keats won the Caldecott Medal for this simple picture book that shows a black child, not as special or as a problem, but as a kid in the neighborhood.

Keene, Carolyn. The Nancy Drew series.

First introduced in 1930, Nancy Drew, with her sporty roadster and nose for mysteries, was a role model for girls during the decades when it seemed like boys had all the fun.

Lenski, Lois. Strawberry Girl. 1945. HarperCollins/Lippincott, $16 (0-397-30109-X); paper, $4.50 (0-06-440585-0).

When this was written, children's literature focused on the experiences of the middle and upper classes. Lenski, in her series of books set in different regions, chose to write about other children: migrant workers, public housing dwellers, backwoods residents. This 1946 Newbery Medal winner tells of a Florida family struggling to make a go of their small farm.

Macaulay, David. Cathedral. 1973. Houghton, paper, $7.95 (0-395-31668-5).

Nonfiction took on a new look when Macaulay's books (beginning with *Cathedral*) appeared on the scene. Instead of just telling about a subject, these books take it apart. A book that is artistic and informative in equal measure.

Maruki, Toshi. Hiroshima No Pika. 1982. Lothrop, $16 (0-688-01297-3).

Should we give children stories about atrocity? The controversy that raged around this picture book continues today, as evidenced by the dispute surrounding the 1995 Caldecott Medal winner, *Smoky Night*.

Pascal, Francine. Sweet Valley High series. Bantam, paper.

Love 'em or hate 'em, there's no doubt that these books changed children's publishing. Never underestimate the power of genre fiction, especially long-running series with familiar characters.

Reflections on a Gift of Watermelon Pickle and Other Modern Verse. Ed. by Stephen Dunning and others. 1966. Lothrop, $18 (0-688-41231-9).

Today's compilers owe a debt of gratitude to the innovative *Reflections*, which proved that it is not only feasible to compile poems with special appeal for YAs but also attractive to a wide audience, particularly when the final package looks dynamic.

Salinger, J. D. The Catcher in the Rye. 1951. Little, Brown, $21.95 (0-316-76953-3); paper, $5 (0-316-76948-7).

Today this would be published as a YA novel. It certainly started a whole genre of first-person stories about lost teenagers trying to find their way in a world of corrupt, weak adults.

Scieszka, Jon. The Stinky Cheese Man and Other Fairly Stupid Tales. Illus. by Lane Smith. 1992. Viking, $16.99 (0-670-84487-X); paper, $5.99 (0-14-055808-0).

This picture book "for all ages," along with Scieszka's *Frog Prince, Continued* (1991), opened wide the floodgates for fractured fairy tales.

Sendak, Maurice. Where the Wild Things Are. 25th anniversary ed. 1988 (orig. pub. 1963). HarperCollins, $15 (0-06-025492-0); paper, $4.95 (0-06-443178-9).

For its candor about children's anger and for the masterful comic energy of its pictures, this launched the contemporary picture book that broke from the view of kids as cute, docile innocents.

Seuss, Dr. Cat in the Hat. 1957. Random, $7.99 (0-394-80001-X).

Using word repetition and easy, fun rhymes, Seuss almost single-handedly started a whole new genre of easy-to-read books.

Tolkien, J. R. R. The Hobbit. (orig. pub. 1938). Many editions available.

A classic fantasy for both adults and children, *The Hobbit*, along with the rest of Tolkien's Middle-Earth saga, stands as a benchmark epic of the struggle between good and evil.

White, E. B. Charlotte's Web. Illus. by Garth Williams. 1952. HarperCollins, $13 (0-06-026385-7); paper, $3.95 (0-06-440055-7).

This all-time favorite fantasy broke from the cutesy animal story to combine humor and longing and a strong sense of character without the slightest condescension in style or story.

Wilder, Laura Ingalls. Little House on the Prairie. Illus. by Garth Williams. 1961. (orig. pub. 1935). HarperCollins, $15.95 (0-06-026446-2); paper, $5 (0-06-080357-6).

There's never been a better blend of history and family stories. The Little House books are not only generational favorites but also led the way for other historical series such as Lovelace's Betsy-Tacy books and Estes' stories about the Moffats.

Zolotow, Charlotte. William's Doll. Illus. by William Pene Du Bois. 1972. HarperCollins, $14.95 (0-06-027047-0); paper, $4.95 (0-06-443067-7).

With her understanding of children's feelings, Zolotow raised a storm about gender roles in her gentle story about a boy who is teased because he wants to play with a doll.

Before Stephen King

by Stephanie Zvirin

Although Stephen King's oeuvre is still out of scope for most middle-graders, lots of fourth-, fifth-, and sixth-grade readers delight in scary tales. These days they have more than ever to choose from, especially in paperback series such as Scholastic's Goosebumps, which they tend to request by number rather than name: "Is number 45 back yet?" As a change of pace from series horror, here's a list of primarily single titles that are filled with enough witches, monsters, and ghosts, in various incarnations, to please even the most die-hard genre fan.

Avi. Something Upstairs: A Tale of Ghosts. 1988. Orchard, o.p.; Avon/Flare, paper, $4.50 (0-380-70853-1).

Gr. 4–6. To set the spirit of a young African American slave to rest, a contemporary boy must travel back in time to 1800.

Ballinger, Erich. Monster Manual: A Complete Guide to Your Favorite Creatures. 1994. Lerner, $19.95 (0-8225-0722-6).

Gr. 5–7. This funny, irreverent, *A-to-Z* of monsters from literature, television, and film is perfect for horror fans who don't *really* want to be scared.

Bellairs, John and **Strickland, Brad.** The Drum, the Doll, the Zombie. 1994. Dial, $14.99 (0-8037-1462-9).

Gr. 5–7. Johnny Dixon and Professor Childermass battle zombies and exorcise voodoo demons invoked by the vicious leader of an evil cult. Just one of many such creepy adventures by Bellairs (and, sometimes, Strickland).

Brown, Roberta Simpson. Queen of the Cold-Blooded Tales. 1993. August House, $19 (0-87483-332-9); paper, $11.95 (0-87483-408-2).

Gr. 5–8. Twenty-three tales that will fill the bill when kids ask for something creepy, gory, and "really scary."

Butler, Beverly. Witch's Fire. 1993. Dutton, $14.99 (0-525-65132-2); Penguin/Puffin, paper, $3.99 (0-14-037614-3).

Gr. 4–6. While still adjusting to her wheelchair and the deaths of her sister and mother, 13-year-old Kirsty finds herself faced with a stepfamily and life in a house that was once the home of a reputed witch.

Byars, Betsy. McMummy. 1993. Viking, $13.99 (0-670-84995-2); Penguin/Puffin, paper, $3.99 (0-14-036439-0).

Gr. 4–6. In this combination of the humorous and the bizarre, a boy faces off against a sinister, humming pea pod that's growing in the greenhouse of a brilliant, eccentric professor.

Coville, Bruce. Goblins in the Castle. 1992. Pocket/Minstrel, paper, $3.99 (0-671-72711-7).

Gr. 5–7. With help from 600-year-old Igor, 11-year-old William ferrets out the shivery secrets of Toad-in-a-Cage Castle.

Creepy Classics: Hair-raising Horror from the Masters of the Macabre. Ed. by Mary Hill. 1994. illus. Random, paper, $4.99 (0-679-86692-2).

Gr. 5–10. Including excerpts from *Frankenstein* and *Macbeth*, these selections from horror classics aren't easy reading, but they're so atmospheric that some middle-graders will be totally enthralled.

Garden, Nancy. My Sister, the Vampire. 1992. Random, o.p.

Gr. 5–7. On their own at their family's summer cottage, 12-year-old Tim and his sisters encounter a series of odd goings-on that lead to the elusive new owners of a nearby deserted island.

Hahn, Mary Downing. Wait till Helen Comes. 1986. Clarion, $14.95 (0-89919-453-2); Avon, paper, $4.50 (0-380-70442-0).

Gr. 5–7. Molly and Michael dislike their new stepsister but realize they must try to save her when a ghost beckons the child to certain doom.

Hamilton, Virginia. The Dark Way: Stories from the Spirit World. 1990. HBJ/Gulliver, $19.95 (0-15-222340-1).

Gr. 4–7. Hamilton retells 24 myths and folktales from around the world, all filled with monsters, devils, and phantoms "eager to leap into the corners of our imaginations."

Herndon, Ernest. The Secret of Lizard Island. 1994. HarperCollins/Zondervan, paper, $5.99 (0-310-38251-3).

Gr. 3–5. When a mix-up sends 12-year-old Eric to the South Pacific on a mission for Wildlife Special Investigations, the boy finds himself on a remote island where scientists seem to be growing 30-foot lizards.

Kehret, Peg. Danger at the Fair. 1995. Dutton/Cobblehill, $14.99 (0-525-65182-9); paper, $4.99 (0-14-037932-0).

Gr. 5–7. Ellen's always wanted to have her fortune told, but what she finds out when she visits the Great Sybil at the county fair spells danger for Ellen and her little brother. A sequel to *Horror at the Haunted House.*

Lehr, Norma. The Secret of the Floating Phantom. 1994. Lerner, $18.95 (0-8225-0736-6).

Gr. 3–6. Eleven-year-old Kathy is more than intuitive. She can actually see things other kids can't—like ghosts who have knowledge of buried treasure.

Maguire, Gregory. Seven Spiders Spinning. 1994. Clarion, $14.95 (0-395-68965-1).

Gr. 4–6. Ice Age spiders thaw out in modern-day Vermont in a neat combination of clever wit and delicious chills.

Mahy, Margaret. The Haunting. 1982. Simon & Schuster/Margaret K. McElderry, $15 (0-689-50243-5).

Gr. 5–7. Barney finds that the ghostly visions and voices he's experiencing are somehow related to an evil uncle with supernatural gifts.

Mazer, Anne. A Sliver of Glass and Other Uncommon Tales. 1996. Hyperion; dist. by Little, Brown, $13.95 (0-7868-0197-2).

Gr. 3–5. Great for reading aloud, these 11 short tales of horror and fantasy are told in an immediate storytelling voice that draws you right into a world both ordinary and fearful.

Owen, Gareth. Rosie No-Name and the Forest of Forgetting. 1996. Holiday, $15.95 (0-8234-1266-0).

Gr. 3–6. Falling through a broken staircase in an old English manor house, 11-year-old Rosie finds she has lost her memory after following a mysterious girl to a nearby forest, where she meets a strange boy and encounters two sinister old women.

Phillips, Ann. A Haunted Year. 1994. Simon & Schuster, $14.95 (0-02-774605-4).

Gr. 4–7. By summoning the spirit of a dead cousin, 11-year-old Florence seems to have loosed a force that's propelling her toward death. A page-turner set in pre–World War I England.

Raw Head, Bloody Bones: African American Tales of the Supernatural. Ed. by Mary E. Lyons. 1991. Scribner, $14 (0-684-19333-7); Aladdin, paper, $3.95 (0-689-80306-0).

Gr. 5–7. This stellar collection of African American supernatural tales includes the expected roundup of ogres and ghosts as well as some lesser-known spirits, among them the Plat-Eye.

Roberts, Willo Davis. Caught! 1994. Atheneum, $14.95 (0-689-31903-7).

Gr. 4–7. When 13-year-old Vickie and her sister arrive at their father's apartment, they find only a photo, a pipe, and wet bloodstains on the carpet.

Ruckman, Ivy. Spell It M-U-R-D-E-R. 1994. Bantam/Skylark, paper, $3.50 (0-553-48175-4).

Gr. 4–6. During a midnight boat escape from their dreadful summer camp, Katy and Andrea hear two men arguing and what sounds like a body being dumped in the lake. Chills and mystery combined.

Schwartz, Alvin. Scary Stories to Tell in the Dark. 1981. illus. HarperCollins, $14.95 (0-397-31926-6); paper, $3.95 (0-06-440170-7).

Gr. 5–8. With genuinely creepy illustrations by Stephen Gammell, this collection of American folklore should be read with the lights on. Schwartz's *More Scary Stories to Tell in the Dark* and *Scary Stories 3* are great follow-ups.

Skurzynski, Gloria. What Happened in Hamelin. 1979. Random, paper, $3.99 (0-679-83645-4).

Gr. 5–7. Browning's famous poem is turned into an evocative story in which the piper Gast rids a German village of rats and then takes its children.

Tolan, Stephanie. Who's There? 1994. Morrow, $15 (0-688-04611-8); paper, $4.95 (0-688-15289-9).

Gr. 5–8. Drew, 14, and her younger brother arrive at the home of their father's estranged family to find a nasty ghost in residence.

Turner, Ann. Rosemary's Witch. 1991. HarperCollins/Charlotte Zolotow, paper, $3.95 (0-06-440494-3).

Gr. 5–8. Nine-year-old Rosemary and her family are happy about moving into a rambling country house, but the fierce, vengeful witch who lived there as a child wants them all out.

Wallace, Bill. Blackwater Swamp. 1994. Holiday, $15.95 (0-8234-1120-6); Minstrel, paper, $3.50 (0-670-51156-4).

Gr. 4–6. New-kid-in-town Ted is glad when Jimmy Watson befriends him—until Jimmy suggests the boys explore Blackwater Swamp to find the house of the witch who's supposed to live there.

Why Am I Grown So Cold? Poems of the Unknowable. Ed. by Myra Cohn Livingston. 1982. Macmillan/Margaret K. McElderry, $14.95 (0-689-50242-7).

Gr. 5–10. These 150 poems from many cultures and centuries speak of spells, sorcerers, phantoms, and monsters.

Wright, Betty Ren. The Ghost Comes Calling. 1994. Scholastic, $14.95 (0-590-47353-0).

Gr. 3–6. Chad likes the rundown cabin his father bought at the lake until he discovers it's haunted by a ghost who doesn't want company.

Young, Richard and **Young, Judy Dockrey**. The Scary Story Reader. 1993. August House, $19 (0-87483-271-3); paper, $11.95 (0-87483-382-5).

Gr. 6–9. The 41 urban legends here are as good for telling around campfires and on sleepovers as they are for reading alone.

Keep on Laughing

by Sally Estes

Laughter is the best medicine, it's said. And who doesn't like a good laugh? Not only that, a good giggle is worth sharing with friends.

Fiction

Avi. "Who Was That Masked Man, Anyway?" 1992. Orchard/Richard Jackson, $14.95 (0-531-05457-8); Avon, paper, $3.99 (0-380-72113-9).

Gr. 5–7. Told entirely through dialogue, this is the story of Frankie Wattleson, who is living out his fantasies through the radio during World War II.

Coville, Bruce. The World's Worst Fairy Godmother. 1996. illus. Pocket/Minstrel, $14 (0-671-00229-5); paper, $3.99 (0-671-00228-7).

Gr. 3–5. It's been one screwup after another for fairy godmother Maybelle Clodnowski; and her boss, who is threatening to take away her wings and wand if she messes up again, offers her a "last chance" assignment.

Danziger, Paula. Forever Amber Brown. 1996. illus. Putnam, $13.95 (0-399-22932-9); paper, $3.50 (0-590-94725-7).

Gr. 2–4. One of the best chapter books about Amber Brown, this is focused and funny as Amber, now in the fourth grade, wonders how much things will change now that Max has proposed to her mother.

Delaney, Michael. Deep Doo-Doo. 1996. Dutton, $14.99 (0-525-45647-3).

Gr. 4–6. When 11-year-old gadget guru Bennet and his best pal, Pete, tinker with an old shortwave transmitter, they soon realize that they can disrupt the transmission of a local TV station, and they interpose the governor's speeches with shots of Pete's dog accompanied by a politically critical voiceover. The tension and hilarity intensify right up to the election.

Dickinson, Peter. Chuck and Danielle. 1996. illus. Delacorte, $14.95 (0-385-32188-0); Dell/Yearling, paper, $3.99 (0-440-41087-5).

Gr. 3–6. This clever, episodic story set in England introduces Danielle and her dog, Chuck, whose funny worldview forms the basis for many laugh-out-loud scenes.

Fleischman, Sid. The 13th Floor: A Ghost Story. 1995. illus. Greenwillow, $15 (0-688-14216-8); Dell/Yearling, paper, $3.99 (0-440-41243-9).

Gr. 4–6. This rollicking ghost story is also a time-travel adventure, with a bit of witchcraft thrown in for good measure, as a ghostly relative from the seventeenth century invokes the help of Bud Stebbens and his attorney sister, Liz.

Franklin, Kristine L. Nerd No More. 1996. Candlewick, $15.99 (1-56402-674-4).

Gr. 4–6. When sixth-grader Wiggie gains unwanted notoriety because his mom hosts a TV science show, he tries on new personalities to rid himself of his nerd image, getting into increasingly more trouble with school officials.

Gutman, Dan. The Kid Who Ran for President. 1996. Scholastic, $15.95 (0-590-93987-4); paper, $3.50 (0-590-93988-2).

Gr. 4–6. In this entertaining romp through the political process, children across the country join 12-year-old Judson Moon's campaign to pressure parents to press for a constitutional amendment abolishing age restrictions for the presidency.

Horvath, Polly. When the Circus Came to Town. 1996. Farrar, $15 (0-374-38308-1).

Gr. 5–8. In this wacky, offbeat novel narrated by fifth-grader Ivy, a small, quiet town becomes divided when some circus folk set down roots—and heaven forbid, decide to enter baked goods in the town's annual bake sale.

James, Mary. Shoebag Returns. 1996. Scholastic, $15.95 (0-590-48711-6).

Gr. 3–6. Shoebag, the cockroach who can magically transform himself into a (yuck!) boy, returns in another off-the-wall Kafkaesque adventure as Shoebag is motivated out of pity for the only boy in a girls' school to become the boy named Stuart Bagg.

Jennings, Patrick. Faith and the Electric Dogs. 1996. illus. Scholastic, $15.95 (0-590-69768-4).

Gr. 3–6. A book with a dog as the narrator is likely to be full of surprises, and this story, in which a faithful Mexican pooch sticks by a sad little girl, is poignant, wonderfully comic, and delightfully unexpected.

Korman, Gordon. The Chicken Doesn't Skate. 1996. Scholastic, $14.95 (0-590-85300-7).

Gr. 4–6. The South Middle School Rangers hockey team is in a serious slump until a wayward chicken named Henrietta, the key ingredient in Milo Neal's science-fair project on the food chain, finds itself sitting on the Rangers' bench. Henrietta's fate hangs in the balance! Korman's *Twinkie Squad* is another slapstick story.

Lynch, Chris. Babes in the Woods. 1997. HarperCollins, lib. ed., $14.89 (0-06-027415-8); paper, $4.50 (0-06-440656-3).

Gr. 5–7. In the title story, *Johnny Chesthair*, and *Scratch and the Sniffs*, the first three entries in the He-Man Women Haters Club series, Lynch hilariously captures the turmoil of boys caught in that awkward limbo between hitting girls and hitting *on* them.

Peck, Richard. Lost in Cyberspace. 1995. Dial, $14.99 (0-8037-1931-0); Penguin, paper, $3.99 (0-14-037856-1).

Gr. 4–7. Who says that humor and sf don't mix? Josh, a sixth-grader who's barely coping with his parents' separation and the stream of unsuitable au pairs his mother hires, at first thinks it's an unwanted complication when his best friend, Aaron, merges two computers into a time machine; let the adventure begin! The sequel is *The Great Interactive Dream Machine* (1996).

Pinkwater, Daniel. Wallpaper from Space. 1996. illus. Simon & Schuster/ Atheneum, $15 (0-689-80764-3).

Gr. 2–4, younger for reading aloud. In this wacky tale, Steven finds that the spaceships on his new wallpaper are not ordinary spaceships but ones piloted by mice who are heading for black holes.

Sanfield, Steve. The Great Turtle Drive. Illus. by Dirk Zimmer. 1996. Knopf, $12 (0-679-85834-2).

Gr. 2–4, younger for reading aloud. A cowboy inspired by a bowl of tasty turtle soup decides to seek his fortune as a turtle drover, and he rounds up 20,000 of the critters, hoping to lead the drive from Texas to Kansas City and sell his herd to Frenchy's Gourmet Eating Establishment and Pizza Parlor. The absurd problems and ingenious solutions will keep children laughing.

Soto, Gary. Off and Running. 1996. illus. Delacorte, $15.95 (0-385-32181-3).

Gr. 3–5. Fifth-graders Miata Ramirez and Ruddy Herrera are running against each other for school president, and the fifth-grade comedy is as lighthearted and affectionate as ever in the book's loosely connected chapters.

Taylor, William. Knitwits. 1992. Scholastic, $13.95 (0-590-45778-0); paper, $2.95 (0-590-45779-9).

Gr. 4–6. The utterly hilarious saga of Charlie Kenney, whose frightful best friend, Alice, bets him he will not be able to knit a sweater for his brother- or sister-to-be. The sequel is Numbskulls (1995).

Vail, Rachel. Do-Over. 1992. Orchard/Richard Jackson, o.p.; Avon, paper, $3.99 (0-380-72180-5).

Gr. 5–9. In a poignant, comical novel, 13-year-old Doug finds out that do-overs are fine in a game of one-on-one, but life is never that simple.

Wynne-Jones, Tim. The Book of Changes. 1995. Orchard/Melanie Kroupa, $15.95 (0-531-09489-8); Penguin, paper, $3.99 (0-14-038071-8).

Gr. 4–7. The dialogue is laugh-out-loud funny in these touching short stories in which the universal situations are drawn right from the middle-grade experience: confronting a bully, starting a first job, learning to lose at sports, discovering weakness in a hero.

Picture Books

Bunting, Eve. Trouble on the T-ball Team. Illus. by Irene Trivas. 1997. Clarion, $13.95 (0-395-66060-2).

Ages 4–7. Something "mysterious" is happening to the members of Linda's T-ball team—everyone is losing something—but why hasn't it happened to Linda yet? What in the world is going on? Another funny read is Bunting's Nasty, Stinky Sneakers (1994).

Choldenko, Gennifer. Moonstruck: The True Story of the Cow Who Jumped over the Moon. Illus. by Paul Yalowitz. 1997. Hyperion; dist. by Little, Brown, $14.95 (0-7868-0158-1).

Ages 5–7. As the horse narrator puts it, Mother Goose got it wrong when she devoted only one line to the cow jumping over the moon—the jump was a major accomplishment, and the horse has the details.

Denim, Sue. The Dumb Bunnies Go to the Zoo. Illus. by Dav Pilkey. 1997. Scholastic/Blue Sky, $13.95 (0-590-84735-X).

Ages 6–8. In their third tale, the Dumb Bunnies have a supremely silly adventure at the zoo when they spot a butterfly hovering around the lion's cage and figure the big cat is loose, and they almost start a riot.

Dewan, Ted. Top Secret. 1997. illus. Doubleday, $15.95 (0-385-32324-7).

Ages 5–7. What happens to the teeth you leave under your pillow at bedtime? Forget the tooth fairy; it's a band of tiny fellows dedicated to the dangerous mission of sneaking into your bedroom and exchanging lost teeth for coins.

Ehrlich, Amy. Parents in the Pigpen, Pigs in the Tub. Illus. by Steven Kellogg. 1993. Dial, $15.99 (0-8037-0933-1); Penguin/Puffin, paper, $5.99 (0-14-056297-4).

Ages 4–8. The farm animals and the farmers decide to trade places, which results in lots of frantic fun and artwork that bubbles out of borders.

Gray, Libba Moore. Is There Room on the Feather Bed? Illus. by Nadine Bernard Westcott. 1997. Orchard/Melanie Kroupa, $16.95 (0-531-30013-7).

Ages 2–6. In the uproarious style of *Never Take a Pig to Lunch* (1994), Westcott's watercolors bring bedlam to the bedroom in Gray's cumulative tale of farmyard animals that come knocking at the door on a rainy night.

Henkes, Kevin. Lilly's Purple Plastic Purse. 1996. illus. Greenwillow, $15 (0-688-12897-1).

Ages 4–6. Lilly, the delightful mousegirl, has started school, and she loves everything about it; most of all, she loves her teacher, Mr. Slinger, so it's only natural that she can't wait to show off her brand-new flashy sunglasses and purple purse to her classmates and teacher, but Mr. Slinger wants Lilly to wait for sharing time.

Karas, G. Brian. I Know an Old Lady. 1995. illus. Scholastic, $14.95 (0-590-46575-9); paper, $1.95 (0-590-02967-3).

Ages 2–6. The popular cumulative nonsense rhyme gets uproarious treatment in a wild picture book with exaggerated, cartoon-style pictures that revel in slapstick action and laconic absurdity.

Koller, Jackie French. No Such Thing. Illus. by Betsy Lewin. 1997. Boyds Mills, $14.95 (1-56397-490-8).

Ages 5–8. From under a bed, a monster mother tells her frightened son, "There are no such things as boys," while similar fright scenes are occurring between a boy and his mother—then boy and monster meet and team up to trick their moms.

Maguire, Gregory. Seven Spiders Spinning. 1994. Clarion, $14.95 (0-395-68965-1).

Gr. 4–6. In a broad farce, seven deadly tarantulas from before the dawn of time invade a contemporary classroom in rural Vermont, where the kids are preparing a Halloween pageant of horrors.

McPhail, David. Pigs Ahoy! 1995. illus. Dutton, $14.99 (0-525-45334-2).

Ages 4–8. This zesty follow-up to *Pigs Aplenty, Pigs Galore* (1993) is set aboard a sparkling cruise ship, where an unsuspecting vacationer finds his cabin "filled with swine. / Some are sitting on a trunk; / The rest are piled up on a bunk."

Meddaugh, Susan. Martha Speaks. 1992. Houghton/Walter Lorraine, $14.95 (0-395-63313-3); paper, $4.95 (0-395-72024-9).

Ages 4–7. When Martha the dog swallows a bowl of alphabet soup, the letters go right to her brain, allowing her to speak—in fact, she won't shut up, much to her family's dismay. Sequels are *Martha Calling* (1994), *Martha Blah Blah* (1996), and *Martha Walks the Dog* (1998).

Naylor, Phyllis Reynolds. The Healing of Texas Jake. 1997. illus. Simon & Schuster/Atheneum, $15 (0-689-81124-1).

Gr. 3–6. In this sequel to *The Grand Escape* (1993), Texas Jake, chief cat in the Club of Mysteries, is recuperating from injuries sustained in a brawl with mastiff Bertram the Bad; and lots of excitement, adventure, and humor ensue as Texas Jake's followers try to help him feel better.

Palatini, Margie. Piggie Pie! Illus. by Howard Fine. 1995. Clarion, $14 (0-395-71691-8); paper, $5.95 (0-395-86618-9).

Ages 5–8. Gritch the witch certainly looks her part, with a pointy hat, a gaptoothed grin, vicious green fingernails, and two beauteous facial moles, as she brooms off to Old MacDonald's Farm in search of eight plump porkers for her favorite pie.

Rathmann, Peggy. Officer Buckle and Gloria. 1995. illus. Putnam, $15.95 (0-399-22616-8).

Ages 4–7. When Officer Buckle visits schools to give safety tips, his presentation gets a slapstick shot of life after he is joined by a police dog named Gloria.

Scieszka, Jon. Math Curse. 1995. Illus. by Lane Smith. Viking, $16.99 (0-670-86194-4).

Ages 6–9. Bold in design, witty in expression, this picture book clearly shows the feelings of frustration, bemusement, panic, and, eventually, triumphant joy that come with the math curse.

Stadler, John. The Cats of Mrs. Calamari. 1997. illus. Orchard/Richard Jackson, $15.95 (0-531-30020-X).

Ages 4–7. Mrs. Calamari has cats, lots of them; her new landlord, Mr. Gangplank, and his dog, Potato, do not like cats, but fortunately, Mr. Gangplank has lost his glasses and doesn't catch on as the cats masquerade as statues, cowboys and cowgirls, or Mrs. Calamari's family members.

Stevens, Janet. Tops and Bottoms. 1995. illus. Harcourt, $15 (0-15-292851-0).

Ages 4–7. Large, dynamic double-page-spread paintings are only part of the charm of this very funny picture book that features appealing, contemporary cousins of Brer Rabbit and Brer Bear, who are involved in a lopsided gardening partnership.

Teague, Mark. The Secret Shortcut. 1996. illus. Scholastic, $14.95 (0-590-67714-4).

Ages 4–8. Wendell and Floyd just can't seem to get to school on time, and, of course, it's never their fault: on Monday, they're delayed by space aliens, on Tuesday, by pirates, and on Wednesday, by a plague of frogs; then they try a secret shortcut that leads to the wildest adventure of all.

Waber, Bernard. A Lion Named Shirley Williamson. 1996. illus. Houghton, $15.95 (0-395-80979-7).

Ages 4–7. Because of a telephone mix-up between a woman at the Wildlife Trading Company and the zoo director, the zoo's new lion is named Shirley Williamson; the other lions are really put out—why are they always taking a backseat to Shirley?

Wells, Rosemary. Bunny Cakes. 1997. illus. Dial, $13.99 (0-8037-2143-9).

Ages 2–6. Max, the determined small rabbit, wants to make an earthworm cake for Grandma's birthday, but his bossy older sister, Ruby, insists that they make an angel surprise cake with raspberry fluff icing. Also check out Bunny Money (1997).

A Moving Experience

by Julie Corsaro

In our mobile society, many kids will move at least once during their early years. Here's a selection of books to share with preschool and elementary grade students to help them deal with and respond to this exciting and scary experience.

Aliki. We Are Best Friends. 1982. illus. Greenwillow lib. ed., $15.93 (0-688-00823-2); paper, $4.95 (0-688-07037-X).

Ages 5–8. Angry and frustrated when his best buddy moves away, Robert eventually lends a hand to new kid Will, who is having adjustment problems of his own.

Blos, Joan. Old Henry. Illus. by Stephen Gammell. 1987. Morrow, lib. ed., $15.93 (0-688-06400-0); paper, $5.95 (0-688-09935-1).

Ages 6–8. Henry moves into and then out of an abandoned house after being pestered by the neighbors about his untidy ways, but both he and the community are later surprised when they miss each other.

Blume, Judy. Then Again, Maybe I Won't. 1971. Simon & Schuster, $14.95 (0-02-711090-7); Dell, paper, $3.99 (0-440-98659-1).

Gr. 5–7. In this frank and sensitive first-person novel, 13-year-old Tony is disturbed by the changes that accompany his family's move to a posh suburb, where his mother becomes a social climber and the "nice" boy next door turns out to be a shoplifter.

Brandenberg, Franz. Nice New Neighbors. Illus. by Aliki. 1977. Greenwillow, $13.88 (0-688-84105-8); paper, $4.95 (0-688-10997-7).

Gr. 1–3. In a rhythmic beginning reader, the kids in a mouse family put on a clever production of "Three Bind Mice," creating roles for their new neighbors, who suddenly become much friendlier.

Cadnum, Michael. The Lost and Found House. Illus. by Steve Johnson and Lou Fancher. 1997. Viking, $15.99 (0-670-84884-0).

Ages 5–8. Moving day is viewed through the eyes of a young boy, his belongings packed, his aquarium emptied of fish, his house vacant, in a story with pictures that work beautifully with the text to convey the boy's longing for what's left behind and his acceptance of what's to come.

Carlson, Nancy. Visit to Grandma's. 1991. illus. Viking, $13.95 (0-670-83288-X); Penguin/Puffin, paper, $4.99 (0-14-054243-4).

Ages 4–7. Tina is upset by the sports car, tap-dancing lessons, and restaurant dining that characterize Grandma Beaver's life since she moved from a farm to a Florida condo.

Caseley, Judith. Jorah's Journal. 1997. illus. Greenwillow, $15 (0-688-14879-4).

Gr. 2–4, younger for reading aloud. Jorah hates having to move from her apartment to a house in a new city, and she uses the journal she gets as a house-warming present to express how she feels ("I hate it here"), but, of course, in the end, she makes a friend and settles in.

Conford, Ellen. Anything for a Friend. 1979. Little, Brown, o.p.; Bantam, paper, $3.50 (0-553-48081-2).

Gr. 5–7. Forced to relocate once again because of her father's corporate job, Wallis is afraid her schoolmates will reject her when they learn she lives in the Tucker house, the site of a recent murder.

Danziger, Paula. Amber Brown Is Not a Crayon. Illus. by Tony Ross. 1994. Putnam, $13.95 (0-399-22509-9); Little, Brown, paper, $3.50 (0-590-45899-X).

Gr. 2–4. When Amber Brown's best friend Justin Daniels and his family are packing up to move away, Justin tries to act as if nothing is happening; Amber picks a fight, and soon the friends aren't speaking.

Hermes, Patricia. Kevin Corbett Eats Flies. Illus. by Carol Newson. 1986. Harcourt, $13.95 (0-15-242290-0); Archway, paper, $2.99 (0-671-69183-X).

Gr. 4–6. In a zesty favorite among middle-grade readers, fly-eater Kevin Corbett and feisty female pal Bailey plan a romantic liaison between their fifth-grade teacher and Kevin's father, who has moved frequently since his wife's death.

Hoff, Syd. Who Will Be My Friends? 1960. illus. HarperCollins, lib. ed., $14.89 (0-06-022556-4); paper, $3.50 (0-06-444072-9).

Ages 5–7. With comic-style artwork, this classic read-alone provides a humorous answer to the question most concerning school-age kids on the move.

Hughes, Shirley. Moving Molly. 1982. illus. Lothrop, lib. ed., $11.88 (0-688-07984-9).

Ages 3–5. Unlike the rest of her busy family, scruffy preschooler Molly is bored with her new home until she explores the vacant lot next door and meets the twins who live in the adjacent house.

Hurwitz, Johanna. Aldo Applesauce. Illus. by John Wallner. 1979. Morrow, lib. ed., $15.93 (0-688-32199-2); Puffin, paper, $3.99 (0-14-034083-1).

Gr. 3–4. Nicknamed Aldo Applesauce by his new classmates during a lunchtime incident, the fourth-grade vegetarian finds a true friend in DeDe, who is having problems of her own accepting her divorced father's absence.

Johnson, Angela. The Leaving Morning. Illus. by David Soman. 1992. Orchard, lib. ed., $15.99 (0-531-08592-9).

Ages 6–8. Striking full-page watercolor paintings and lyrical prose capture the bittersweet experiences of an African American family as they say farewell to friends and relatives in their urban neighborhood.

Johnston, Tony. The Quilt Story. Illus. by Tomie dePaola. 1992. Putnam, $15.95 (0-399-21009-1); paper, $5.95 (0-399-22403-3).

Ages 5–8. A quilt lovingly stitched by her mother comforts a pioneer girl when her family moves to the frontier; the same quilt comforts another girl several generations later when her family leaves the old house for a new one.

Keats, Ezra Jack. The Trip. 1978. illus. Greenwillow, lib. ed., $15.93 (0-688-84123-6); paper, $4.95 (0-688-07328-X).

Ages 5–8. In a richly imaginative story featuring a familiar hero and collage illustrations, Louie uses a handmade diorama to pretend he's back in his old neighborhood on Halloween.

Komaiko, Leah. Annie Bananie. Illus. by Laura Cornell. 1987. HarperCollins, $15 (0-06-023259-5); paper, $4.95 (0-06-441398-3).

Ages 4–7. Jaunty drawings are the

ideal foil for this rhyming story in which the narrator remembers the offbeat influence she and constant companion Annie Bananie had on each other ("Made her grow a half inch taller / Shrunk her ears / Made both feet smaller").

Lexau, Joan. Rooftop Mystery. Illus. by Syd Hoff. 1968. HarperCollins, lib. ed., $14.89 (0-06-023865-8).

Gr. 1–3. Embarrassed that he has to carry his sister's large doll to a new apartment, Sam and best friend Albert solve a mystery when the cherished toy disappears from a city rooftop.

Lowry, Lois. Anastasia Again! Illus. by Diane DeGroat. 1981. Houghton, $15 (0-395-31147-0); Bantam, paper, $3.99 (0-440-40009-0).

Gr. 4–7. This witty and poignant sequel to *Anastasia Krupnik* finds the precocious 12-year-old strongly against a move to suburbia until she becomes enamored with a large, old Victorian house that has a tower room just for her.

Mitsumasa, Anno. Anno's Counting House. 1982. illus. Putnam, $15.95 (0-399-20896-8).

Ages 4–8. Ingeniously incorporating such mathematical concepts as odd and even numbers, simple sets and subsets, and addition and subtraction, the beautiful and intricate drawings show what happens when 10 little people move from one house to another.

Namioka, Lensey. Yang the Youngest and His Terrible Ear. 1992. Illus. by Kees de Kiefte. Little Brown, $15.95 (0-316-59701-5); Dell, paper, $3.99 (0-440-40917-9).

Gr. 3–5. In a warm and humorous story, nine-year-old Yingtao, whose family has recently moved from Shanghai to Seattle, struggles with the English language, confusing customs, and being tone deaf in a family of talented musicians.

O'Donnell, Elizabeth. Maggie Doesn't Want to Move. Illus. by Amy Schwartz. 1987. Simon & Schuster, lib. ed., $15 (0-02-768830-5); paper, $3.95 (0-688-08405-2).

Ages 5–8. Telling anyone who will listen that his baby sister, Maggie, doesn't want to move, Simon feels better (and Maggie, too) once he meets a friendly classmate and his new male teacher.

Park, Barbara. The Kid in the Red Jacket. 1987. Knopf, lib. ed., $13.99 (0-394-98189-8); paper, $3.99 (0-394-80571-2).

Gr. 3–5. In a funny and popular book, sixth-grader Howard fears that the sad but pesky first-grader from across the street will ruin his budding friendship with the local boys in his new community.

Rogers, Fred. Moving. 1987. illus. Putnam, o.p.

Ages 3–5. In a reassuring tone, a familiar TV personality tells young kids what they can expect to happen when they move, how they can help out, and the different feelings they might experience.

Rosen, Michael. Moving. Illus. by Sophy Williams. 1993. Viking, $12.99 (0-670-84865-4).

Ages 5–8. In a story told from a cat's perspective, the soft, striking pastel drawings capture the mysterious quality ("I am nowhere and everywhere") of a poem about moving from one house to another.

Schulman, Janet. The Big Hello. Illus. by Lillian Hoban. 1976. Greenwillow, o.p.; Mulberry, paper, $3.95 (0-688-08405-2).

Gr. 1–2. An airplane ride, a lost doll, a shaggy new dog, and a neighbor who has been to Disneyland five times distinguish Sara's early days in California.

Schwartz, Amy. Mrs. Moskowitz and the Sabbath Candles. 1983. illus. Jewish Publication Society, paper, $6.95 (0-8276-0231-6).

Ages 5–8. The warm memories associated with an old pair of Shabbat candles help Mrs. Moskovitz settle into her new apartment as she prepares a Sabbath meal for family and friends.

Sharmat, Marjorie. Gila Monsters Meet You at the Airport. Illus. by Byron Barton. 1980. Simon & Schuster, $14.95 (0-02-782450-0); Aladdin, paper, $4.95 (0-689-71383-5).

Ages 5–8. Convinced he'll have to chase buffalo, wear a 10-gallon hat, and ride a horse to school, a young New Yorker moving out west reconsiders such notions after he meets a boy at the airport with like-minded misconceptions about the new life that awaits him in the East.

Slote, Alfred. Moving In. 1988. Harper-Collins, o.p.

Gr. 5–7. Eleven-year-old Robby Miller is even more upset about his family's move to the Midwest when he meets Ruth Lowenfeld, a woman his widowed father is enamored of and whom Robby doesn't like.

Stevenson, James. No Friends. 1986. illus. Greenwillow, lib. ed., $12.88 (0-688-06507-4).

Ages 5–8. When Louie and Mary Ann are afraid they won't make any friends in their new neighborhood, Grandpa (in his usual fashion) tells them a nonsensical tale of mysterious bullies and bouncing brothers that accompanied his childhood move.

Stolz, Mary. King Emmett the Second. Illus. by Garth Williams. 1991. Greenwillow, $12.95 (0-688-09520-8).

Gr. 2–4. In a story that has convincing characters and situations, a young city boy named Emmett adapts (albeit, after a few temper tantrums) to life in the country and the death of his pet pig, King Emmett.

Thesman, Jean. Nothing Grows Here. 1994. HarperCollins, $14 (0-06-024457-7).

Gr. 4–6. Twelve-year-old Maryanne misses the house she lived in with her parents as well as her old friends; most of all, though, she misses her father, who died suddenly of a heart attack, and the days she worked with him in the garden.

Tobias, Tobi. Moving Day. Illus. by William Pene Du Bois. 1976. Knopf, o.p.

Ages 4–6. Du Bois' small, exquisite drawings help the young narrator explain how her teddy bear feels about the ups and downs of relocating from one house to another ("Bear's a little scared / not me").

Waber, Bernard. Ira Says Good-bye. 1988. illus. Houghton, $14.95 (0-395-48315-8); paper, $5.95 (0-395-58413-2).

Ages 5–8. Ira doesn't realize how upset his best chum is about moving away until Reggie lets down his brave front and the boys make prompt arrangements for a weekend visit.

First Mysteries

by Stephanie Zvirin

Encyclopedia Brown, Cam Jansen, Nate the Great, and Nancy Drew (who has graduated to college sleuthing in the Nancy Drew on Campus series) have been doing their amateur sleuthing long and successfully enough to prove that there are more than a few kids who relish a good mystery. The following list, which includes a sampling of old and new single titles as well as selected series entries, can provide new mystery readers not only with an introduction to the genre but also hours of fun.

Young Readers

Adler, David. Cam Jansen and the Ghostly Mystery. 1996. illus. Viking, $11.99 (0-670-86872-8).

Gr. 2–4. Amateur sleuth Cam Jansen puts her photographic memory to work when a ticket booth is robbed by someone dressed as a ghost.

Ahlberg, Allan. Mystery Tour. Illus. by André Amstutz. 1991. Greenwillow, $12.95 (0-688-09957-2).

Gr. 2. Funnybones characters Big Skeleton, Little Skeleton, and Dog Skeleton come across some mysterious dark shapes, the identities of which beginning readers will enjoy guessing.

Allard, Harry. Miss Nelson Is Missing. Illus. by James Marshall. 1977. Houghton, $15 (0-395-25296-2); paper, $4.95 (0-395-40146-1).

Gr. 1–3. A joke and a gentle mystery combine in a sprightly picture book in which a rabble-rousing class finds its beloved teacher Miss Nelson suddenly replaced by witchy Miss Viola Swamp.

Christelow, Eileen. Gertrude, the Bulldog Detective. 1992. illus. Clarion, $13.95 (0-395-58701-8).

Ages 5–8. Canines Roger and Mabel send their sleuthing friend Gertrude B.

Dog on a wild-goose chase to teach her a lesson.

Clifford, Eth. Flatfoot Fox and the Case of the Missing Schoolhouse. Illus. by Brian Lies. 1997. Houghton, $13.95 (0-395-81446-4).

Gr. 2–3. The latest in the series finds Wacky Weasel taking credit for making the local school disappear and Flatfoot Fox uncovering the truth in the best Sherlock Holmes tradition.

Cushman, Doug. Aunt Eater's Mystery Vacation. 1992. illus. HarperCollins, $14.95 (0-06-020513-X); paper, $3.50 (0-06-444169-5).

Gr. 1–2. A series of "real-life" mysteries interrupts amateur detective Aunt Eater's relaxing holiday.

Cushman, Doug. Mystery of King Karfu. 1996. illus. HarperCollins, $14.95 (0-06-024796-7).

Gr. 2–4. King Karfu's famous stone chicken has disappeared, and wombat detective Seymour Sleuth and his rodent sidekick Abbott Muggs are on the case.

Howe, James. Hot Fudge. Illus. by Leslie Morrill. 1990. Morrow, $13.95 (0-688-08237-8); Avon, paper, $5.99 (0-380-70610-5).

Ages. 4–8. What's happening to the

fudge? Harold the dog and Chester the cat solve the mystery.

Hurd, Thatcher. Art Dog. 1996. illus. HarperCollins, $14.95 (0-06-024424-0).

Ages 4–8. Who stole the famous Mona Woofa from the Dogopolis Museum of Art? Mild-mannered museum guide Arthur, disguised as Art Dog, smells out the missing picture.

Levy, Elizabeth. The Karate Class Mystery: Invisible Ink. Illus. by Denise Brunkus. 1996. Scholastic, paper, $3.99 (0-590-60323-X).

Gr. 2–4. When Justin's karate belt is stolen, the three grade-school friends in the Invisible Inc. trio go to work.

Maifair, Linda L. The Case of the Bashed-Up Bicycle. 1996. Zondervan, paper, $3.99 (0-310-20736-3).

Gr. 2–4. Likable Darcy Doyle gets right on the case when her brother's new bike is stripped.

Murphy, Elspeth Campbell. The Mystery of the Eagle Feather. Illus by Joe Nordstrom. 1995. Bethany, paper, $3.99 (1-55661-413-6).

Gr. 2–4. While visiting Timothy's Indian pen pal, cousins Timothy, Titus, and Sarah-Jane track down a thief who is stealing precious eagle feathers from ceremonial garb.

Naylor, Phyllis Reynolds. Ducks Disappearing. Illus. by Tony Maddox. 1997. Simon & Schuster/Atheneum, $13 (0-689-31902-9).

Ages 2–5. A toddler plays detective after noticing that the number of ducklings in a group he sees marching proudly across the courtyard gets smaller each time he looks.

Roth, Susan. Creak, Thump, Bonk! illus. 1995. Simon & Schuster, $13 (0-689-80290-0).

Ages 3–5. Three adventurous boys and a dog undertake a bit of amateur

detecting to determine the cause of some mysterious nighttime noises.

Sharmat, Marjorie Weinman and **Sharmat, Craig.** Nate the Great and the Tardy Tortoise. Illus. by Marc Simont. 1995. Delacorte, $13.95 (0-385-32111-2); Dell, paper, $3.99 (0-440-41269-2).

Gr. 1–3. As with others in the series, this beginning reader has both style and humor as it follows Nate the Great's attempts to help a tortoise find its way home.

Supraner, Robyn. Sam Sunday and the Mystery at the Ocean Beach Hotel. Illus. by Will Hillenbrand. 1996. Viking, $14.99 (0-670-84797-6).

Ages 6–8. Detective Sam Sunday rises to the challenge when a mysterious caller beckons him to the Ocean Beach Hotel.

Middle Readers

Avi. Windcatcher. 1991. Simon & Schuster, $14 (0-02-707761-6); Avon, paper, $4.50 (0-380-71805-7).

Gr. 4–7. In a combination mystery and adventure story, 11-year-old Tony's sailing adventures are spiced with the tantalizing promise of buried treasure and the dangerous interference of a couple of crooks.

Bailey, Linda. How Can I Be a Detective If I Have to Baby-Sit? 1996. Albert Whitman, $13.95 (0-8075-3404-8); paper, $4.50 (0-8075-3405-6).

Gr. 4–6. Stevie Diamond does her share of botching things up when she investigates some strange goings-on at a mountain camp where she's baby-sitting.

Bellairs, John. House with a Clock in Its Walls. Illus. by Edward Gorey. 1993. Penguin/Puffin, paper, $3.99 (0-14-036336-X).

Gr. 4–6. The first book in a fine series of mystery-fantasy adventures finds newly orphaned 10-year-old Lewis puzzling over odd ticking noises in the walls of his uncle Jonathan's old mansion.

Bunting, Eve. Coffin on a Case. 1992. HarperCollins, $13.95 (0-06-020273-4); paper, $4.50 (0-06-440461-7).

Gr. 4–6. Twelve-year-old Henry Coffin, the son of a private detective, exercises his own sleuthing skills when he's hired by a teenager to find her missing mother.

Byars, Betsy. The Dark Stairs: A Herculeah Jones Mystery. 1994. Viking, $13.99 (0-670-85487-5).

Gr. 4–6. The first and best of a series, this introduces two quirky amateur sleuths: bossy, obstreperous, snoopy Herculeah and her bumbling sidekick Meat.

Carris, Joan D. Beware the Ravens, Aunt Morbelia. 1995. Little, Brown, $14.95 (0-316-12961-5).

Gr. 4–7. Cliff-hanging chapters mark the latest Aunt Morbelia adventure, in which Todd, Jeff, and Aunt Morbelia travel to London to an eerie manor house that Aunt Morbelia has inherited.

Christian, Mary Blount. Sebastian (Super Sleuth) and the Copycat Crime. 1993. illus. Simon & Schuster, lib. ed., $13 (0-02-718211-8).

Gr. 3–5. When a manuscript is stolen at a mystery writers' conference, canine Sebastian and his human partner John must untangle the clues.

Curry, Jane Louise. The Great Smith House Hustle. 1993. Simon & Schuster/ Margaret K. McElderry, $14.95 (0-689-50580-9).

Gr. 4–6. The Smith children smell a rat when a savings-and-loan company claims their grandmother's house.

Hildick, E. W. The Case of the Wiggling Wig. 1996. illus. Simon & Schuster, $15 (0-689-80082-7).

Gr. 4–6. A broken leg doesn't stop McGurk, who decides that the old lady down the block is really a man in disguise and sends his investigative cohorts out to find the truth. Latest in a popular series.

Howe, James. Dew Drop Dead. 1990. Simon & Schuster/Atheneum, $14 (0-689-31425-6); Avon, paper, $4.50 (0-380-71301-2).

Gr. 5–7. When Sebastian and his friends explore an abandoned inn, they're shocked to discover a corpse in one of the rooms.

Kehret, Peg. Frightmares: Don't Go Near Mrs. Tallie. 1995. Pocket/Minstrel, $14 (0-671-89192-8); paper, $3.99 (0-671-89191-X).

Gr. 3–6. Finding a home for Mrs. Tallie's cat seems like a perfect project for Care Club members, until the woman's suddenly deteriorating health calls up the question of poison.

Medearis, Angela. The Spray-Paint Mystery. 1996. illus. Scholastic/Apple, paper, $2.99 (0-590-48474-5).

Gr. 3–5. Like a veteran detective, third-grader Cameron collects evidence, questions suspects, and examines motives until he finds out who's been spray painting a wall at the school.

Naylor, Phyllis Reynolds. The Bomb in the Bessledorf Bus Depot. 1996. Simon & Schuster/Atheneum, $15 (0-689-80461-X); Aladdin, $3.99 (0-689-80599-3).

Gr. 4–6. Who is responsible for the Middleburg bombings? Eleven-year-old Bernie Bessledorf thinks it's either his revenge-seeking sister or his secretive brother. Part of an entertaining series.

Osborne, Mary Pope. Spider Kane and the Mystery at Jumbo Nightcrawler's. Illus. by Victoria Chess. 1993. Knopf/ Borzoi, $14 (0-679-80856-6); paper, $3.50 (0-679-85393-6).

Gr. 3–5. When he discovers his initials have been forged and some gold is missing from the ant colony, arachnid Spider Kane uses his musical talent and his sleuthing experience to negotiate a web of insect intrigue.

Quackenbush, Robert. Evil under the Sea: A Miss Mallard Mystery. 1992. illus. Pippin, $15.95 (0-945912-16-1).

Gr. 2–4. Intrepid Miss Mallard, ducktective extraordinaire, confronts a slew of suspects while trying to determine who is destroying the coral in the Great Barrier Reef.

Raskin, Ellen. The Westing Game. 1978. Dutton, $15.99 (0-525-42320-6); Penguin/Puffin, paper, $4.99 (0-14-034991-X).

Gr. 5–6. Thirteen-year-old Tabitha-Ruth is in the thick of things after an eccentric millionaire requires his 16 heirs to follow a series of intriguing clues before claiming their inheritance. Awarded the Newbery Medal.

Roberts, Willo Davis. Absolutely True Story: My Trip to Yellowstone Park with the Terrible Rupes (No Names Have Been Changed to Protect the Guilty) by Lewis Q. Dodge. 1994. Simon & Schuster/Atheneum, $15 (0-689-31939-8); paper, $3.99 (0-689-81464-X).

Gr. 4–7. As much slapstick as mystery, this still offers a few nice twists and mysterious turns, including a kidnapping and some bumbling thieves.

Sobol, Donald J. Encyclopedia Brown and the Case of Pablo's Nose. 1996. illus. Doubleday, $14.95 (0-385-32184-8); paper, $3.99 (0-553-48513-X).

Gr. 3–6. Idaville's Encyclopedia Brown has been around a long time as far as mystery readers are concerned, but he hasn't lost his knack for crime solving, as this last round of short mysteries proves.

Wallace, Barbara Brooks. Cousins in the Castle. 1996. Simon & Schuster/Atheneum, $15 (0-689-80637-X).

Gr. 4–6. In a period mystery filled with dastardly doings and firm friendships, orphan Amelia Fairchild leaves the Victorian London she knows for a new home in America with distant relatives she's never met.

Before Oliver Twist

by Ilene Cooper

Unique characters, dramatic settings, mysterious goings-on—these are the hallmarks of Charles Dickens' works. Kids whose reading skills are not yet up to Dickens can still relish the atmospheric pleasures of a Dickensian style in these novels written with verve and spirit.

Aiken, Joan. The Wolves of Willoughby Chase. 1963. Doubleday, o.p.; Dell, paper $4.50 (0-440-49603-9).

Gr. 5–8. An English country house is the setting for this Victorian drama that has delighted children for decades.

Alexander, Lloyd. Westmark. 1981. Dutton, $15.95 (0-525-42335-4); Dell, paper, $3.99 (0-440-99731-3).

Gr. 5–8. Young Theo, a printer's apprentice, befriends a lost princess in this marvelously full-bodied adventure story.

Avi. Beyond the Western Sea: The Escape from Home. 1996. Orchard/Richard Jackson, $18.95 (0-531-09513-4).

Gr. 6–10. This pulsing 1850s emigrant adventure is packed with action and a huge cast of villains and heroes in the Liverpool slums, all desperate to get on a ship bound for America. Book 2 in the Beyond the Western Sea saga is *Lord Kirkli's Money* (1996).

Avi. The Man Who Was Poe. 1991. Avon, paper $4.50 (0-380-71192-3).

Gr. 6–9. A brother and a sister left alone are aided by an unexpected source—Edgar Allen Poe, in the guise of his fictional detective, Auguste Dupin.

Avi. The True Confessions of Charlotte Doyle. 1990. illus. Orchard/Richard Jackson, $16.95 (0-531-05893-X); Avon, paper, $4.50 (0-380-71475-2).

Gr. 6–9. A 13-year-old girl finds herself the sole female passenger on a rickety ship with a cutthroat captain and a mutinous crew.

Babbitt, Natalie. Goody Hall. 1986. illus. Farrar, paper, $4.95 (0-374-42767-4).

Gr. 4–6. An ornate house is shrouded in mystery and surrounded by legends of a costumed robber.

Burnett, Frances Hodgson. The Secret Garden. 1909. Many editions available.

Gr. 4–6. The classic story of the haughty orphan Mary, her spoiled cousin, Colin, and Dickon, the boy who loves animals, all of whom are transformed by a secret garden.

Dickens, Charles. A Christmas Carol. Illus. by Trina Schart Hyman. 1983. Holiday, $16.95 (0-8234-0486-2).

Gr. 6–9. Because it is not a full-length novel, this is one of Dickens' offerings that younger readers should be able to handle. The perennial favorite is handsomely illustrated here by Hyman's rich colorplates.

Doherty, Berlie. Street Child. 1994. Orchard, $15.95 (0-531-06864-1); Penguin/Puffin, paper, $4.99 (0-14-037936-3).

Gr. 5–8. At times very bleak, this story of an orphan boy roaming the streets of Victorian London paints an honest picture of life at the time.

Fleischman, Paul. Saturnalia. 1990. HarperCollins/Charlotte Zolotow, $14.95 (0-06-021912-2); paper, $4.50 (0-06-447089-X).

Gr. 7–10. Although set earlier than Dickens' stories, this tale of the festival in which servants and masters trade places boasts the same verve and fascinating cast of characters.

Fleischman, Sid. The Whipping Boy. Illus. by Peter Sis. 1986. Greenwillow, lib. ed., $16 (0-688-06216-4); Troll, paper, $3.95 (0-8167-1038-4).

Gr. 3–6. Jemmy, an orphan plucked from the streets, becomes the designated whipping boy for a nasty prince—but eventually the two run away together.

Garfield, Leon. The Empty Sleeve. 1988. Delacorte, o.p.

Gr. 5–8. Set in eighteenth-century England, this is the story of twins born at a bad-luck hour. Garfield ably blends moral lessons with suspense.

Newman, Robert. The Case of the Baker Street Irregular. 1984. Simon & Schuster/Aladdin, paper, $4.95 (0-689-70766-5).

Gr. 4–6. This book and its companion, The Case of the Vanishing Corpse (1980), are atmospheric mysteries that use Sherlock Holmes' London to good advantage.

Parks, Ruth. Playing Beatie Bow. 1982. Simon & Schuster/Atheneum, lib. ed., $14.95 (0-689-30889-2); Penguin/Puffin, paper, $3.99 (0-14-031460-1).

Gr. 6–9. Set in Australia, this affecting time-travel story brings 14-year-old Abby back to Victorian Sydney, where she finds her life intertwined with the Bows, a family of candy makers.

Pearce, Philippa. Tom's Midnight Garden. 1986. HarperCollins/Lippincott, $13.89 (0-397-30477-3); paper, $4.95 (0-06-440445-5).

Gr. 4–6. In this much-beloved time-travel story, Tom meets a girl from Victorian times in a magic garden.

Pullman, Philip. The Ruby in the Smoke. 1987. Knopf, lib. ed., $11.99 (0-394-98826-4); paper, $4.99 (0-394-89589-4).

Gr. 8–10. Sixteen-year-old Sally Lockhart becomes involved in a deadly web of events as she searches London for a mysterious ruby.

Stanley, Diane and **Vennena, Peter.** Charles Dickens: The Man Who Had Great Expectations. Illus. by Diane Stanley. 1993. Morrow, $15 (0-688-09110-5).

Gr. 3–8. For those intrigued by the fiction on this list, here's the story of the man who started it all.

Twain, Mark. The Prince and the Pauper. 1881. Many editions available.

Gr. 6–9. The story of a prince who changes places with his poor subject continues to be a favorite scenario for young people.

Wallace, Barbara Brooks. The Twin in the Tavern. 1993. Simon & Schuster/Atheneum, lib. ed., $15 (0-689-31846-4); paper, $3.95 (0-689-80167-X).

Gr. 4–6. In this jaunty Dickensian story with delightful characters and plenty of twists and turns to keep you guessing, young Taddy is left an orphan and, afraid it's the workhouse for him, accompanies rough Neezer and his dolt of a companion, who had stopped by to rob the house.

Let's Read a Poem

by Sally Estes

Here's a gathering of poems that are fun, that may be about the ordinary or the extraordinary, or that are rooted in various cultures. Try some on for size.

Berry, James. Everywhere Faces Everywhere. 1997. illus. Simon & Schuster, $16 (0-689-80996-4).

Gr. 6–10. These 46 poems by a Jamaican writer now living in England celebrate nature, observe cultural conflict, welcome and salute diversity, and celebrate love as the recurring opportunity for redemption.

Burleigh, Robert. Hoops. Illus. by Stephen T. Johnson. Harcourt/Silver Whistle, $16 (0-15-201450-0).

Gr. 4–8. In a strong, spare poem celebrating the way it feels to play basketball, Burleigh re-creates motion in poetry from the player's point of view. Johnson's deeply shaded, impressionistic illustrations express the players' moves and emotions as they show older teens playing the game on an outside court, shooting at a netless rim.

A Caribbean Dozen: Poems from Caribbean Poets. Ed. by John Agard and Grace Nichols. Illus. by Cathie Felstead. 1994. Candlewick, $19.95 (1-56402-339-7).

Gr. 4–6, younger for reading aloud. This bright, colorful anthology offers 55 poems by 13 gifted poets from the English-speaking Caribbean that are deeply rooted in the details of West Indian culture.

Celebrate America: In Poetry and Art. Ed. by Nora Panzer. 1994. illus. Hyperion; dist. by Little, Brown, $18.95 (1-56282-664-6).

Gr. 4–7. Illustrated with paintings, sculpture, drawings, and photographs from the National Museum of American Art at the Smithsonian, the poems in this diverse collection celebrate the country's landscape, its melting-pot makeup, city and rural life, history, and pastimes.

Dakos, Kalli. The Goof Who Invented Homework and Other School Poems. 1996. illus. Dial, $13.99 (0-8037-1927-2).

Gr. 3–6. The down-to-earth poems in this collection range in tone from funny and frustrated to sad and profound as they explore the nitty-gritty of life in an elementary school as experienced by the students, the teachers, and even the desks.

Extra Innings: Baseball Poems. Ed. by Lee Bennett Hopkins. Illus. by Scott Medlock. 1993. Harcourt, $16 (0-15-226833-2).

Gr. 4–6. May Swenson, Lillian Morrison, Ernest Thayer, and editor Hopkins are among the poets who give their own personal takes on the art and craft of baseball in these 19 poems, which are bolstered by vibrant, eye-catching illustrations.

Fletcher, Ralph. Ordinary Things: Poems from a Walk in Early Spring. 1997. illus. Simon & Schuster/Atheneum, $15 (0-689-81035-0).

Gr. 4–6, younger for reading aloud. Observations on ordinary things reveal more complex thoughts and emotions.

The 33 poems in *I Am Wings: Poems about Love* (1994) make up a kind of short story about a boy falling in and out of love.

George, Kristine O'Connell. The Great Frog Race and Other Poems. 1997. Clarion, $14.95 (0-395-77607-4).

Gr. 4–6, younger for reading aloud. The words in these enticing poems illustrated with rich, warm-toned oil paintings capture children throwing water balloons, hovering over pollywogs in a shallow pond, listening to Canada geese flying overhead.

Hughes, Langston. The Dream Keeper and Other Poems. Illus. by Brian Pinkney. 1994. Knopf, $13 (0-679-84421-X).

Gr. 4–12. A handsome edition of Hughes' classic poetry collection, originally published in 1932, includes seven additional poems and Pinkney's signature scratchboard illustrations that express the emotion and the beat of the poetry, which is as powerful today as it was some 60 years ago.

I Thought I'd Take My Rat to School: Poems for September to June. Ed. by Dorothy M. Kennedy. Illus. by Abby Carter. 1993. Little, Brown, $16.95 (0-316-48893-3).

Gr. 2–5. There's nothing sentimental about these 57 poems that reflect children's experiences with school, from classroom to recess to homework and from frustration to bemusement to humor.

Lear, Edward. There Was an Old Man: A Gallery of Nonsense Rhymes. Illus. by Michèle Lemieux. 1994. Morrow, $15 (0-688-10788-5).

Gr. 3–5, younger for reading aloud. Fifty-three of Lear's comical limericks appear, each on a single page or a double-page spread, accompanied by watercolors only slightly more surreal than the verse. A veritable feast of the absurd in verse and illustrations.

Levy, Constance. When Whales Exhale and Other Poems. 1996. illus. Simon & Schuster/Margaret K. McElderry, $15 (0-689-80946-8).

Gr. 3–5, younger for reading aloud. Levy makes us see small things within the sweep of ocean, land, and sky in these deceptively casual poems that project images from the child's physical experience. Another collection by Levy is *A Tree Place and Other Poems* (1994).

Livingston, Myra Cohn. Cricket Never Does: A Collection of Haiku and Tanka. 1997. illus. Simon & Schuster/Margaret K. McElderry, $15 (0-689-81123-3).

Gr. 5–8. In more than 60 small pieces, Livingston captures the spirit of seasonal change, evoking a sense of delight in each stage of the year, from spring ("Look how the birds turn / the telephone lines / into a musical staff!") to winter ("These are not foaming / white horses, but only waves / in a wild ocean"). In *Flights of Fancy and Other Poems* (1994), Livingston leaps from the mundane to the imaginary.

Prelutsky, Jack. A Pizza the Size of the Sun. Illus. by James Stevenson. 1996. Greenwillow, $18 (0-688-13235-9).

Gr. 3–6. Prelutsky uses verbal sleight of hand to create another magical anthology of light verse that ranges from a display of elegance and wit to a delight in wordplay, all finding perfect visual expression in Stevenson's witty ink drawings.

Roll Along: Poems on Wheels. Ed. by Myra Cohn Livingston. 1993. Simon & Schuster/Margaret K. McElderry, $11.95 (0-689-50585-X).

Gr. 3–5, much younger for reading aloud. The exhilaration of being on wheels is celebrated, whether the wheels are on the bikes and skateboards that kids ride themselves or on the cars, buses, trucks, and trains that they travel in and watch and dream about.

Schwartz, Alvin. And the Green Grass Grew All Around: Folk Poetry from Everyone. Illus. by Sue Truesdell. 1992. HarperCollins, $15 (0-06-022757-5).

Gr. 3–6. With exuberant multicultural cartoon drawings on every page, this joyful roundup of folk poetry—from skip-rope rhymes and stories to jokes and riddles—is a collection everyone will delight in sharing.

Silverstein, Shel. Falling Up. illus. HarperCollins, $16.95 (0-06-024802-5).

Gr. 3–6. Well worth the wait, this great new collection of poems tickles the funny bone while it slips in some food for thought.

Slam Dunk: Poems about Basketball. Ed. by Lillian Morrison. 1995. illus. Hyperion; dist. by Little, Brown, $15.89 (0-7868-2042-X); paper, $5.95 (0-7868-1060-2).

Gr. 4–6. In a choice collection for those who find poetry in basketball but don't expect to find basketball in poetry, Morrison showcases 42 short poems by the likes of Mel Glenn, Eloise Greenfield, Walter Dean Myers, Jack Prelutsky, and Mary Swenson. Morrison also compiled *At the Crack of the Bat* (1992) for baseball fans.

Soto, Gary. Canto Familiar. 1995. illus. Harcourt, $17 (0-15-200067-4).

Gr. 4–6. A companion to Soto's *Neighborhood Odes* (1992), this collection of simple free verse captures common childhood moments at home, at school, and in the street.

Steig, Jeanne. Alpha Beta Chowder. Illus. by William Steig. 1992. HarperCollins/Michael di Capua, $15 (0-06-205006-0).

Gr. 4–8. Joy in words, their sound and meaning, the more esoteric the better—that's the basis of this collection of mock-heroic nonsense verses illustrated in pen-and-watercolor illustrations that range from sly to wild.

Stevenson, James. Sweet Corn. 1995. illus. Greenwillow, $15 (0-688-12647-2).

Gr. 3–5, younger for reading aloud. Stevenson's concrete poems tell and show how BIG KIDS ALWAYS SIT IN THE FRONT SEAT to see what's coming; little kids get stuck in the back and never see anything till it's over.

This Same Sky: A Collection of Poems from around the World. Ed. by Naomi Shihab Nye. 1992. illus. Simon & Schuster/Four Winds, $17 (0-02-768440-7); Aladdin, paper, $8.99 (0-689-80630-2).

Gr. 7–12. In casual, colloquial translations, contemporary poets from 68 countries shatter the idea of poetry as being something special and exotic.

Wong, Janet S. Good Luck Gold and Other Poems. 1994. Simon & Schuster/Margaret K. McElderry, $14 (0-689-50617-1).

Gr. 3–5. Fresh, honest, and not at all reverential, these poems are simple dramatic monologues about growing up Asian American.

The God Squad

by Ilene Cooper

Many children have an intense interest in religion, not only their own but that of others. This bibliography highlights some of the best of recent religious fiction and nonfiction, along with some not-to-be missed earlier ones.

Armstrong, Carole. Lives and Legends of the Saints: With Paintings from the Great Art Museums of the World. 1995. Simon & Schuster, $17 (0-689-80277-3).

Gr. 4–7, slightly younger for reading aloud. Children intrigued by the lives of the saints will relish this beautifully illustrated volume that contains paintings from museums such as the Louvre and the National Gallery.

Blume, Judy. Are You There God? It's Me, Margaret. 1970. Simon & Schuster, $15 (0-02-710991-7); Dell/Yearling, paper, $3.99 (0-440-90419-6).

Gr. 5–7. Margaret, the daughter of a Jewish-Protestant union, has all sorts of questions about her role in the world; so she asks God.

Cormier, Robert. Other Bells for Us to Ring. 1990. Delacorte, $15 (0-385-30245-2); Dell/Yearling, paper, $3.99 (0-440-40717-6).

Gr. 4–6. A Catholic girl and a Unitarian girl become friends, despite the difference in their religions.

Demi. Buddha Stories. 1996. illus. Holt, $16.95 (0-8050-4886-3).

Gr. 3–6, younger for reading aloud. In an elegant presentation of 10 of Demi's favorite *jakatas*, or Buddha's stories, the one-page tales are told in the fashion of Aesop's fables and are enhanced by drawings done in gold ink on dark navy blue pages. Demi tells the story of Siddhartha's childhood and follows his path to enlightenment in *Buddha* (1996).

dePaola, Tomie. The Miracles of Jesus. 1987. illus. Holiday, $16.95 (0-8234-0635-0); paper, $8.95 (0-8234-1211-3).

Ages 5–8. Twelve miracles are introduced and handsomely illustrated in this companion to *The Parables of Jesus*. In *Mary: The Mother of Jesus* (1995), dePaola tells the story of Mary's life with joyful reverence and simple yet majestic artwork.

Douglas, Kirk. The Broken Mirror. 1997. Simon & Schuster, $13 (0-689-81493-3).

Gr. 5–10. In a spare novella, actor Kirk Douglas tells the story of a Jewish child who denies his identity and loses his faith when everyone he loves is killed in the Holocaust.

Fishman, Cathy Goldberg. On Passover. Illus. by Melanie W. Hall. 1997. Simon & Schuster/Atheneum, $16 (0-689-80528-4).

Ages 4–7. A young girl who asks questions as her family gets ready for Passover is shown that the holiday incorporates all the senses—she sees the seder plate, smells the soup and other foods, feels the silk matzo cover, and hears the Passover service read from the Haggadah.

Gellman, Marc and **Hartman, Thomas.** How Do You Spell God? Answers to Big Questions from around the World. 1995. Morrow, $16 (0-688-13041-0); paper, $5.95 (0-688-15296-1).

Gr. 5–9. Arranged to link rather than separate religions, this down-to-earth book will make kids think about God.

Gerstein, Mordicai. The Mountains of Tibet. 1987. illus. HarperCollins, $14.95 (0-06-022144-5); paper, $5.95 (0-06-443211-4).

Ages 6–8. A very simple story that introduces the concept of reincarnation to young children.

Ghazi, Suhaib Hamid. Ramadan. Illus. by Omar Rayyan. 1996. Holiday, $15.95 (0-8234-1254-7); paper, $6.95 (0-5234-1275-X).

Ages 5–9. With his family, young Hakeem watches for the new moon that signals the beginning of the month of Ramadan and then joins the 28-day period of fasting and prayer.

Goldin, Barbara Diamond. Bat Mitzvah: A Jewish Girl's Coming of Age. 1995. illus. Viking, paper, $5.99 (0-14-037516-3).

Gr. 5–7. Explaining the ancient Jewish rituals and describing how women's roles in many congregations are still evolving, Goldin tells participants what to expect at a bat mitzvah.

Grimes, Nikki. Come Sunday. Illus. by Michael Bryant. 1996. Eerdmans, $15 (0-8028-5108-8); paper, $7.50 (0-8028-5134-7).

Ages 4–8. At church, La Tasha is filled with Sunday spirit, and both Grimes' poetry and Bryant's exuberant illustrations capture her joy.

Herman, Charlotte. What Happened to Heather Hopkowitz? 1994. Jewish Publication Society, $8.95 (0-8276-0520-X).

Gr. 4-6. Heather Hopkowitz decides to become a more observant Jew, and her new orthodoxy affects lives other than her own.

Jackson, Dave and **Jackson, Neta.** The Betrayer's Fortune. 1994. illus. Bethany House, paper, $5.99 (1-55661-467-5).

Gr. 3–6. A teenager's struggle to reestablish his trust in God is the focus of a novel set in the early 1500s during the persecution of the Anabaptists (later to become the Mennonites).

Kerr, M. E. What I Really Think of You. 1982. HarperCollins, paper, $3.50 (0-06-447062-8).

Gr. 7–9. Several of Kerr's novels deal with the subject of religion. Here, the daughter of a Holy Roller preacher and the son of a celebrated televangelist are brought together.

Kimmel, Eric. Bar Mitzvah: A Jewish Boy's Coming of Age. 1995. illus. Viking, $15 (0-670-85540-5),

Gr. 4–7. A fine introduction to the Jewish male's coming-of-age ceremony. A companion to Bat Mitzvah by Barbara Diamond Goldin (1995).

Kroll, Virginia L. I Wanted to Know All about God. Illus. by Debra R. Jenkins. 1994. Eerdmans, $15 (0-8028-5078-2).

Ages 5–8. Children ask simple questions about God: What does God do in the morning? What colors does he like?

Lamstein, Sarah Marwil. Annie's Shabbat. Illus. by Cecily Lang. 1997. Albert Whitman, $15.95 (0-8075-0376-2).

Ages 4–7. A warm first-person story captures the essence of the Jewish Sabbath as young Annie describes what her household is like from sundown on Friday to Saturday night when the first three stars appear in the sky.

L'Engle, Madeleine. The Glorious Impossible. 1990. illus. Simon & Schuster, $22 (0-671-68690-9).

Gr. 6–9. Using Giotto's frescoes and the New Testament as the basis of her text, L'Engle introduces readers to the Glorious Impossible—the forging of divinity and humanity in Jesus.

Le Tord, Bijou. Peace on Earth: A Book of Prayers from around the World. 1992. illus. Doubleday, $18 (0-385-30692-X).

Ages 4–6. With her usual simplicity and charm, Le Tord follows children around the world through a prayerful day.

Lewin, Ted. Sacred River. 1995. illus. Clarion, $14.95 (0-395-69846-4).

Gr. 2–4. Set on the Ganges, this beautifully illustrated book shows how millions of Hindu pilgrims come to the river to purify their souls.

Madhu Bazaz, Wangu. Hinduism. 1991. illus. Facts On File, $17.95 (0-8160-2447-2).

Gr. 6–9. Part of the World Religions series, this offers a detailed look at an ancient religion.

Maifair, Linda Lee. Batter Up, Bailey Benson! 1997. illus. Zondervan, paper, $3.99 (0-310-20705-3).

Gr. 3–5. This and Maifair's *Go Figure, Gavbriella Grant!*, both from the Winners Series, feature girls who try to live by their Christian principles as they pursue their favorite sports.

Mark, Jan. God's Story. Illus. by David Parkins. 1998. Candlewick, $17.99 (0-7636-0376-7).

Gr. 6–9. Mark's telling of the familiar biblical tales about Adam and Eve, Noah, Abraham, Moses, and David is fresh, is sometimes funny, and has an air of immediacy that brings the stories right into the life of modern-day readers.

McDonough, Yona Z. Eve and Her Sisters: Women of the Old Testament. Illus. by Malchah Zeldis. 1994. Greenwillow, $15 (0-688-12512-3).

Ages 5–9. Fourteen women of the Bible are introduced in an attractive picture book.

Morpurgo, Michael. The War of Jenkins' Ear. 1995. Putnam/Philomel, $16.95 (0-399-22735-0).

Gr. 6–9. Set at a British boarding school in the early 1950s, this is the thought-provoking story of Toby Jenkins, who's astonished to find himself chosen as the disciple of a new boy, Christopher, who believes himself to be the reincarnation of Jesus Christ.

Oberman, Sheldon. The Always Prayer Shawl. Illus. by Ted Lewin. 1994. Boyds Mills, $14.95 (1-878093-22-3); Penguin, paper, $5.99 (0-14-038214-3).

Ages 6–9. A moving story about a prayer shawl, called a *tallis* in Hebrew, that is passed down from father to son.

Paterson, Katherine. Who Am I? 1992. illus. Eerdmans, paper, $9.95 (0-8028-5072-3).

Gr. 5–7. A forthright religious book that helps young people assess their place in the world.

Rogasky, Barbara. The Golem. Illus. by Trina Schart Hyman. 1996. Holiday, $18.95 (0-8234-0964-3).

Gr. 4–6, younger for reading aloud. Rogasky tells the story with a colloquial warmth and a Yiddish idiom, portraying everything from the rabbi in his book-filled library to the golem rampaging through the streets of Prague, all illustrated with a depth of perception, a sense of character, and an exquisite detail of line.

Rosen, Michael. Elijah's Angel. Illus. by Aminah Robinson. 1992. Harcourt, $14 (0-15-225394-7).

Gr. 3–6. A Jewish boy worries that by accepting a carved wooden angel from a Christian friend, he will be doing something against his religion.

Roth, Susan L. Buddha. 1994. illus. Doubleday, $15.95 (0-385-31072-2).

Ages 6–9. This picture book for older children follows the life of Siddhartha. Extraordinary collage art illustrates the story.

Rylant, Cynthia. A Fine White Dust. 1986. Bradbury, $15 (0-02-777240-3); Aladdin, paper, $3.95 (0-689-80462-8).

Gr. 5–8. The visit of a traveling preacher man gives 13-year-old Peter impetus to resolve his own religious conflicts.

Sasso, Sandy E. God's Paintbrush. Illus. by Annette Compton. 1992. Jewish Lights, $16.95 (1-879045-22-2).

Ages 4–8. In simple language and with naive art, this book explores the questions little children have about God. Also by Sasso, *But God Remembered: Stories of Women from Creation to the Promised Land* (1995) and *A Prayer for the Earth: The Story of Naamah, Noah's Wife* (1997).

Schnur, Steven. The Tie Man's Miracle: A Chanukah Tale. Illus. by Stephen T. Johnson. Morrow, $16 (0-688-13463-7).

Ages 5–8. Hanukkah, the Jewish celebration of miracles, is a wonderfully fitting backdrop for the sentimental but beautifully told story of a peddler whose family was lost in the Holocaust.

Speare, Elizabeth G. The Bronze Bow. 1961. Houghton, $16 (0-395-07113-5); paper, $7.95 (0-395-13719-5).

Gr. 6–9. The story of a young Jewish rebel against Rome who is attracted by the teachings of Jesus.

Taylor, Sydney. All-of-a-Kind Family. Illus. by Helen John. 1951. Peter Smith, repr., $17.75 (0-8446-6253-4); Dell, paper, $4.50 (0-440-40059-7).

Gr. 3–6. The first entry in a heartfelt, often amusing series that incorporates Jewish life at the turn of the century.

Winthrop, Elizabeth. He Is Risen: The Easter Story. Illus. by Charles Mikolaycak. 1985. Holiday, lib. ed., $15.95 (0-8234-0547-8).

Gr. 2 and up. A handsomely illustrated version of the Easter story.

Wisniewski, David. Golem. 1996. illus. Clarion, $15.95 (0-395-72618-2).

Gr. 3–6. Extraordinary cut-paper collages show and tell the stark, terrifying legend of the giant monster of sixteenth-century Prague, who was created by a rabbi to protect his people in the ghetto against racist persecution.

Wormser, Richard. American Islam: Growing Up Muslim in America. 1994. Walker, $16.95 (0-8027-8343-0).

Gr. 6–10. One of the few books about Islam and the only one that describes the lives of American teens who follow this religion.

Yolen, Jane. O Jerusalem. Illus. by John Thompson. 1996. Scholastic/Blue Sky, $15.95 (0-590-48426-5).

Gr. 4–6, younger for reading aloud. Yolen captures the feelings of Judaism, Christianity, and Islam toward Jerusalem in her poetry, and Thompson brings her words to life in exquisite paintings.

Young, Ed. Genesis. 1997. illus. HarperCollins/Laura Geringer, $16.95 (0-06-025356-8).

Ages 5–8. Based on the King James Version of Genesis, this picture book interprets the Creation story through familiar words and impressionistic artwork, providing a distinctive vision of the Creation.

Cliff-Hangers

by Sally Estes

Experience the adventurous trials and tribulations of those who survive disaster from the comfort of your own armchair. What to read after the now-classic *Hatchet*, by Gary Paulsen, or *Julie of the Wolves*, by Jean Craighead George, or *Island of the Blue Dolphins*, by Scott O'Dell? Here are some suggestions.

Avi. The Barn. 1994. Orchard/Richard Jackson, $13.95 (0-531-06861-7); Avon, paper, $4.50 (0-380-72562-2).

Gr. 4–8. Set in the Oregon Territory during the 1850s, this is a classic survival story about kids who suddenly find themselves on their own without adults to care for them.

Byars, Betsy. Tornado. illus. HarperCollins, $13.95 (0-06-026449-7); paper, $3.95 (0-06-442063-9).

Gr. 3–5. When a tornado is sighted, a boy's family rushes to the storm cellar, where, anxious about the father who's still in the cornfield, they listen to the storm overhead and to the stories related by their farmhand, Pete, about Tornado, the dog he loved as a boy.

Campbell, Eric. The Place of Lions. 1991. Harcourt, $15.95 (0-15-262408-2).

Gr. 6–9. When their small plane crashes over the Serengeti, injuring his father and the pilot, Chris Harris begins a lesson in desert survival, as he's surrounded and threatened by a pride of lions.

Cottonwood, Joe. Quake! 1995. Scholastic, $13.95 (0-590-22232-5); paper, $3.50 (0-590-22233-3).

Gr. 5–8. In a story based on California's 1989 earthquake, Cottonwood chronicles the nightmarish ordeal through the eyes of 14-year-old Fran, who's home with her bratty brother, Sidney, and a friend while her parents attend the World Series game.

Easley, Maryann. I Am the Ice Worm. 1996. Boyds Mills, $15.95 (1-56397-412-6).

Gr. 4–6. Californian Alison Atwood is radically out of her element when an airplane crash leaves her stranded in Alaska, where, rescued by a passing Inupiat, she soon finds herself isolated by cultural differences.

Finley, Mary Pearce. Soaring Eagle. 1993. Simon & Schuster, $14 (0-671-75598-6).

Gr. 5–9. On a dangerous journey from their Mexican village to Bent's Fort, Colorado, in 1845, Julio's father is killed by Apaches, and Julio, injured and without provisions, is finally rescued by the Cheyenne, who teach him their ways.

Harrah, Madge. My Brother, My Enemy. 1997. Simon & Schuster, $16 (0-689-80968-9).

Gr. 4–7. Fourteen-year-old Robert Bradford must make his own way in the world after a Susquehannock war party massacres his family and burns their cabin, barn, and tobacco shed in Virginia in the 1670s.

Hill, Kirkpatrick. Toughboy and Sister. 1990. Simon & Schuster, $15 (0-689-50506-X); Penguin/Puffin, paper, $3.99 (0-14-034866-2).

Gr. 4–6. When their father dies, now orphaned Toughboy and Sister, Alaskan Athbascan Indians, are alone at their summer family fishing camp and must learn to survive through trial and error until their eventual rescue. The dramatic sequel is *Winter Camp* (1993).

Kehret, Peg. Night of Fear. 1994. Dutton/Cobblehill, $14.99 (0-525-65136-5); Pocket, paper, $3.99 (0-671-89217-7).

Gr. 6–10. After he's abducted by a man who fits the description of a wanted bank robber, T. J. makes numerous unsuccessful escape attempts before finding out that his creepy captor is actually a pyromaniac bent on revenge.

Mahy, Margaret. Underrunners. 1992. Viking, $14 (0-670-84179-X).

Gr. 5–7. Two kids on a wild New Zealand peninsula try to escape a stalker who is elegant, crazy, and violent—and who turns out to be a close relative.

Myers, Edward. Climb or Die. 1994. Hyperion; dist. by Little, Brown, $14.95 (0-7868-0026-7); paper, $4.95 (0-7868-1129-3).

Gr. 6–9. When the family car careens off a slippery Rocky Mountain road in a blinding snowstorm, injuring both parents, it's up to Danielle, 14, and Jake, 13, to scale nearby Mount Remington to get help from the weather station.

Napoli, Donna Jo. Trouble on the Tracks. 1996. Scholastic, $14.95 (0-590-13447-7).

Gr. 5–7. Two Americans, Zach, 13, and his younger sister, Eve, are thrown off a train speeding across the Australian desert after they encounter two bumbling, dangerous smugglers.

Naylor, Phyllis Reynolds. The Fear Place. 1994. Simon & Schuster/Atheneum, $16 (0-689-31866-9); paper, $3.95 (0-689-80442-3).

Gr. 5–7. Set in a remote area of the Rocky Mountains, this is a cliff-hanger about Doug Brillo, 12, who overcomes his terror of heights to rescue the older brother he hates.

Paterson, Katherine. Jip, His Story. 1996. Dutton/Lodestar, $15.99 (0-525-67543-4).

Gr. 5–9. In a story of an orphan boy in Vermont in the 1850s, Paterson has taken the old foundling story and made it new, laying bare the dark historical truth about slavery juxtaposed against the transforming light of love.

Paulsen, Gary. Brian's Winter. 1996. Delacorte, $15.95 (0-385-32198-8).

Gr. 5–9. In this sequel to *Hatchet* (1987), Paulsen spins out an alternative ending: What if 13-year-old Brian hadn't been rescued before winter came? What if he had had to face the cold months alone in the Canadian north?

Peterson, P. J. White Water. 1997. Simon & Schuster, $15 (0-689-80664-7).

Gr. 4–6. Apprehensive about being on the white-water river in the first place, wimpy Greg suddenly finds himself in charge when his father is bitten by a rattlesnake.

Smith, Roland. Thunder Cave. 1995. Hyperion; dist. by Little, Brown, $16.95 (0-7868-0068-2); paper, $5.95 (0-7868-1159-5).

Gr. 5–8. While searching for his wildlife biologist father in the Kenyan bush, 14-year-old Jacob Lansa joins forces with Supeet, a young Masai on a quest, and the boys encounter a dangerous ring of poachers.

Across Time: Time-Travel Tales

by Sally Estes

Time travel is a perennial favorite with readers, and those whose appetites have been whetted by the likes of Madeleine L'Engle's *A Wrinkle in Time* and its many sequels/companions, Nancy Bond's *Another Shore*, Jane Yolen's *Devil's Arithmetic*, Ruth Park's *Playing Beatie Bow*, and Alan Garner's *Red Shift* may find these more recent titles also to their liking.

Alcock, Vivien. The Red-Eared Ghosts. 1997. Houghton, $15.95 (0-614-28825-8).

Gr. 5–7. Mary Frewin can see ghosts, but the red-eared people she sees are actually on the other side of a time warp, where she makes her way to learn about her great-great-grandmother, who mysteriously disappeared.

Barron, T. A. The Ancient One. 1992. Putnam/Philomel, $17.95 (0-399-21899-8); Tor; dist. by St. Martin's, paper, $4.99 (0-8125-3654-1).

Gr. 6–9. In a fantasy with a strong environmental message, 13-year-old Kate is thrust back in time, where she meets a member of an Indian tribe that vanished centuries earlier and soon finds herself fighting to save the forest, not only in her time but also in the distant past. Companion novels are *Heartlight* (1990) and *The Merlin Effect* (1994).

Blair, Margaret Whitman. Brothers at War. 1997. White Mane, paper, $7.95 (1-57249-049-7).

Gr. 4–7. While participating in a Civil War battle reenactment, Rob and Jamie Henry and the object of their affections, Sarah Singleton, find themselves transported back to the real battle—the brothers on opposite sides and Sarah as an assistant to Clara Barton.

Burgess, Melvin. An Angel for May. 1995. Simon & Schuster, $15 (0-671-89004-2).

Gr. 5–8. When troubled 12-year-old Tam travels 50 years into the past with the homeless Rosey, whom he encountered in some deserted ruins near his small English town, he meets Rosey as a young girl and struggles to help her.

Chetwin, Grace. Collidescope. 1990. Simon & Schuster/Bradbury, o.p.

Gr. 7–10. The lives of three individuals—Hahn, a humanoid android from the future; contemporary teenage girl Frankie; and 15-year-old Sky-Fire-Trail, from a time almost 1,500 years earlier—collide when Hahn's surveying mission goes askew.

Chetwin, Grace. Friends in Time. 1992. Simon & Schuster/Bradbury, o.p.

Gr. 4–7. When lonely 12-year-old Emma Gibson wishes for just one real friend, she finds herself face to face with Abigail Bentley, a 10-year-old who has arrived from 1846, and tries to keep Abigail in the present time in a plan that backfires and sends both girls back to an invisible limbo in Abigail's time.

Cooney, Caroline B. Both Sides of Time. 1995. Delacorte, $10.95 (0-385-32174-0); Dell, paper, $4.50 (0-440-21932-9).

Gr. 6–10. Ripe for romance, Annie

Lockwood finds it when she falls 100 years into the past and meets the family that lived in the once-elegant mansion in her hometown. The sequels are *Out of Time* (1996) and *Prisoner of Time* (1998).

Cresswell, Helen. The Watchers: A Mystery at Alton Towers. 1994. Simon & Schuster, $15.95 (0-02-725371-6).

Gr. 4–6. Escaping a children's home, Katy and Josh hide out in a huge nearby amusement park, where the local bag lady is someone—or something—else at sundown, and Katy's thrill at learning how to travel through time is tempered by the knowledge that children in another dimension are counting on her to destroy the evil force that haunts the park.

Curry, Jane Louise. Moon Window. 1996. Simon & Schuster/Margaret K. McElderry, $16 (0-689-80945-X).

Gr. 5–8. Packed off to stay at Winterbloom with an elderly cousin, Joellen bolts out the round attic window and finds herself back in time, where she meets several ancestors and uncovers a secret room, its supernatural inhabitant, and family secrets.

French, Jackie. Somewhere around the Corner. 1995. Holt, $14.95 (0-8050-3889-2).

Gr. 4–7. Terrified by a baton-wielding policeman at a 1994 rowdy demonstration in Sydney, Australia, Barbara takes an old man's advice and imagines herself walking around a corner to a safe place where she finds herself in 1932 Sydney.

Griffin, Peni R. 1993. Switching Well. Macmillan/ Margaret K. McElderry, $16 (0-689-50581-7); Penguin/Puffin, $4.99 (0-14-036910-4).

Gr. 5–9. In a clever, funny, and touching story, two 12-year-olds who live in San Antonio (Ada in 1891 and Amber in 1991) find themselves switch-

ing places when each asks a favor of a wish-granting fairy who lives in an old well—Ada to live 100 years in the future and Amber 100 years in the past.

Hahn, Mary Downing. Time for Andrew: A Ghost Story. 1994. Clarion, $15 (0-395-66556-6); Avon, paper, $4.50 (0-380-72469-3).

Gr. 4–6. Spending the summer at his great-aunt Blythe's ancestral house, shy Drew unwittingly opens a door to the past and travels back to 1910, where he changes places with his brash distant relative, Andrew, who looks just like him.

Hildick, E. W. The Case of the Weeping Witch: A McGurk Fantasy. 1992. Macmillian, $15 (0-02-743785-X).

Gr. 3–7. In this McGurk episode, time travel takes the gang of young sleuths to seventeenth-century New England to rescue Hester Bidgood, accused of witchcraft.

Jordan, Sherryl. The Juniper Game. 1991. Scholastic, $13.95 (0-590-44728-9); paper, $3.50 (0-590-44729-7).

Gr. 7–9. Participating in a telepathic experiment with Juniper Golding, his lab partner, 14-year-old Dylan Pidgely finds himself back in the fifteenth century, where he and Juniper become dangerously enmeshed in the life of an accused witch.

Lindbergh, Anne. Nick of Time. 1994. Little, Brown, $15.95 (0-316-52629-0).

Gr. 7–9. When 14-year-old Jericho and his best friend, Alison, meet Nick, a boy who has come from the year 2094, they follow him to find out what life in the future holds.

Lindbergh, Anne. Three Lives to Live. 1992. Little, Brown, $14.95 (0-316-52628-2); Pocket/Minstrel, paper, $3.50 (0-671-86732-6).

Gr. 6–8. Compelled to explain the

mysterious arrival of her "twin," Daisy (who came down the laundry chute), 13-year-old Garet Atkins eventually discovers that the chute is a conduit through time and that she, her grandmother, and Daisy are all the same person.

Lyon, George Ella. Here and Then. 1994. Orchard/Richard Jackson, $15.95 (0-531-06866-8); Troll, paper, $3.95 (0-8167-4207-3).

Gr. 6–8. While playing the part of Eliza Hoskins, a woman who nursed the wounded from both North and South, in a Civil War reenactment, seventh-grader Abby "becomes" Eliza, hearing her thoughts in her head, writing Eliza's words in her journal, even going back in time to experience Eliza's life firsthand.

MacGrory, Yvonne. The Secret of the Ruby Ring. 1994. illus. Milkweed, $14.95 (0-915943-88-3); paper, $6.95 (0-915943-92-1).

Gr. 4–6. When 11-year-old Lucy receives from her grandmother a ruby ring with the power to grant two wishes, Lucy, who wishes to live in a "much larger house," finds herself transported to a nearby castle in a time long past, 1885.

McKay, Hilary. The Amber Cat. 1997. Simon & Schuster/Margaret K. McElderry, $15 (0-689-81360-0).

Gr. 4–6. In this sequel to *Dog Friday* (1995), tales of a long-ago summer and a mysterious girl named Harriet become intertwined with the present day as Robin Brogan and his friend Dan listen to Mrs. Brogan's tales while recuperating from chicken pox.

Peck, Richard. Voices after Midnight. 1989. Delacorte, $14.95 (0-385-29779-3); Dell, paper, $4.50 (0-440-40378-2).

Gr. 6–9. Moving into a 100-year-old Manhattan town house with a mysterious history, 14-year-old Chad, his younger brother, Luke, and his 16-year-old sister, Heidi, find themselves involved with the house's inhabitants from the previous century and being pulled toward a specific event of March 12, 1888.

Reiss, Kathryn. Time Windows. 1991. Harcourt, $16 (0-15-288205-7); Scholastic, paper, $3.50 (0-590-46536-8).

Gr. 6–9. When 13-year-old Miranda finds a dollhouse in her attic, she discovers that through the dollhouse's attic windows she can see past events in the lives of an eight-year-old girl in 1904 and two brothers in the 1940s, and in piercing together the disparate stories, discovers the house has infected generations of women with psychologically abusive behavior. Miranda also appears in *Pale Phoenix* (1994).

Scieszka, Jon. Tut, Tut. Illus. by Lane Smith. 1996. Viking, $11.99 (0-670-84832-8).

Gr. 4–6. High jinks reign in this Time Warp Trio adventure, which finds the friends in the heart of ancient Egypt, where they square off against a pharaoh's evil priest as they search for the all-important Book, Joe's little sister, and Cleo the cat. Other madcap tales include *Your Mother Was a Neanderthal* (1993) and *The Time Warp Trio 2095* (1995).

Scott, Deborah. The Kid Who Got Zapped through Time. 1997. Avon, $14 (0-380-97356-1).

Gr. 4–7. When "Flattop" Kincaid gets a new computer game that entails touching a small purple glass to a wizard's hand on the screen, he is propelled back to twelfth-century England, where his lack of knowledge about medieval customs and society leads him not only into trouble but also heroism.

Service, Pamela F. Storm at the Edge of Time. 1994. Walker, $16.95 (0-8027-8306-6).

Gr. 4–6. When a dark storm gathers

force at the edge of time, the Neolithic mage Urkar recruits help to stem it from three of his descendants: Arni, a Viking lad; Jamie, a modern American girl; and Tyaak, a boy from the future.

Sleator, William. Strange Attractors. 1989. Dutton, $13.95 (0-525-44530-7); Penguin/Puffin, paper, $4.99 (0-14-034582-5).

Gr. 7–10. After waking up from an attack of amnesia and finding in his pocket a strange object that turns out to be a time-travel phaser, top science student Max finds himself being hunted by a father and daughter and their ruthless look-alikes from another time line, all of whom want the phaser.

Slepian, Jan. Back to Before. 1993. Putnam/Philomel, $14.95 (0-399-22011-9); Scholastic, paper, $3.25 (0-590-48459-1).

Gr. 5–7. In an unusual and compelling story, 11-year-old Linny and his cousin Hilary suddenly find themselves in their Brooklyn neighborhood a year earlier in time and shortly before Linny's mother dies and Hilary's idolized father walks out. Can they make things turn out better this time?

Sterman, Betsy and **Sterman, Samuel.** Backyard Dragon. Illus. by David Wenzel. 1993. HarperCollins, $14 (0-06-020783-3).

Gr. 3–5. Wyrdryn, a fifteenth-century Welsh dragon, is banished by the wizare Gwilym to Kings Ridge, New Jersey, and the twentiegth century, and when young Owen discovers the dragon, no one believes in its existence.

Vick, Helen Hughes. Walker of Time. 1993. Harbinger House, paper, $9.95 (0-943173-80-9).

Gr. 6–10. When they enter a sacred cave, Walker, a 15-year-old Hopi, and Tag, the 12-year-old son of a field archaeologist, are blasted back in time 750 years to the Sinagua Indian settlement, which is threatened with destruction. The sequel is *Walker's Journey Home* (1995).

Wesley, Mary. Haphazard House. 1993. Overlook; dist. by Viking, $14.95 (0-87951-470-1).

Gr. 5–7. When an eccentric artist and his family buy a run-down estate house in the English countryside, they discover that, at Haphazard House, time itself runs haphazardly.

Winthrop, Elizabeth. The Battle for the Castle. 1993. Holiday, $15.95 (0-8234-1010-2); Dell, paper, $4.50 (0-440-40942-X).

Gr. 4–7. In a sequel to *The Castle in the Attic* (1985), William once again enters the castle in the attic and is whisked back to medieval times, where he finds himself caught up in a wild drama involving an ancient chant that foretells the return of evil.

Woodruff, Elvira. Orphan of Ellis Island: A Time Travel Adventure. 1997. Scholastic, $14.95 (0-590-48245-9).

Gr. 4–7. Accidentally left behind on a fifth-grade school trip to Ellis Island, lonely orphan Dominic finds himself transported back to a village in southern Italy, where he's accepted into a poor family that teaches him what it's truly like to be hungry and poor.

How the West Was Won—
in Children's Books

by Hazel Rochman and Sally Estes

This bibliography draws together just a few of the great children's books that have opened up the history of the West. Here are true adventures, biographies, and tall tales, as well as accounts of daily hardship and survival, stories of women, men, and children. Yet there are many people whose voices have not yet been heard.

Picture Books

Goble, Paul. Death of the Iron Horse. 1987. illus. Bradbury, o.p.; Aladdin, paper, $4.95 (0-689-71686-9).

Ages. 5–7. A melancholy tale of rail sabotage from the point of view of the young Cheyennes who caused it. Other great picture books by Goble include *Love Flute* (1992), a love story rooted in an exquisite legend of the Plains Indians, and *Buffalo Woman* (1984), another myth of the Great Plains Indians.

Harvey, Brett. Cassie's Journey: Going West in the 1860s. Illus. by Deborah Kogan Ray. 1988. Holiday, $15.95 (0-8234-0684-9); paper, $6.95 (0-8234-1172-9).

Gr. 2–4. A child's personal story of hardship and survival as her family migrates westward is illustrated with impressionistic pictures in graphite pencil. Historical fiction in picture-book format.

Lyon, George Ella. Dreamplace. Illus. by Peter Catalanotto. 1993. Orchard, $15.95 (0-531-05466-7); paper, $6.95 (0-531-07101-4).

Ages 4–8. With other tourists, a young girl sees the 800-year-old site of the Anasazi as it is today, dreams of it as it was when the tribe lived there, and imagines their suffering when drought forced them to leave. A richly atmospheric evocation of dual realities.

Pinkney, Andrea D. Bill Pickett: Rodeo-Ridin' Cowboy. Illus. by Brian Pinkney. 1996. Harcourt/Gulliver, $16 (0-15-200100-X).

Ages 4–8. Told with verve, relish, and just enough of a cowboy twang, the Pinkneys' lively, illustrated biography of the famous black rodeo star also includes an excellent overview of the history of rodeos and black cowboys.

Rounds, Glen. Sod Houses on the Great Plains. 1995. illus. Holiday, $15.95 (0-8243-1162-1); paper, $6.95 (0-8234-1263-6).

Ages 5–8. With his strong, craggy drawings and effective writing, Rounds not only shows what the earthen houses looked like and how they were built but also lets you feel what they were like as homes.

Say, Allen. Grandfather's Journey. 1993. illus. Houghton, $16.95 (0-395-57035-2).

Ages 6–8, older for reading alone.

Winner of the 1994 Caldecott Medal, this is an exquisitely illustrated account of the restless journey of an early Japanese American immigrant who came to California and always felt caught between his new home and the one he left behind.

Stanley, Diane. Saving Sweetness. Illus. by G. Brian Karas. 1996. Putnam, $15.95 (0-399-22645-1).

Ages 4–8. A few great villains, an endearingly foolish sheriff, and a resourceful, loving heroine are the ingredients in a fresh and funny western tale written in a folksy narrative style.

Teague, Mark. How I Spent My Summer Vacation. 1995. illus. Crown, $16 (0-517-59998-8).

Ages 5–7. Wallace Bleff's unsuspecting teacher gets more than she bargained for when the quiet student erupts in glee as he reads his essay on his summer vacation—a wild and woolly Old West adventure that bursts from his paper into full-color, action-packed double-spread paintings.

Van Leeuwen, Jean. A Fourth of July on the Plains. Illus. by Henri Sorensen. 1997. Dial, $14.99 (0-8037-1771-7).

Ages 4–8. Based on a diary account of a July Fourth celebration on the Oregon Trail in 1852, this combines a child's voice and viewpoint with handsome paintings that capture the pioneer experience.

Wright, Courtni C. Wagon Train: A Family Goes West in 1865. Illus. by Gershom Griffith. 1995. Holiday, $15.95 (0-8234-1152-4).

Gr. 3–5, younger for reading aloud. Finding themselves unwelcome on the big wagon trains heading west in 1865, Ginny, a young African American girl, and her family form their own group of newly freed friends and relatives for the dangerous journey.

Nonfiction

Axelrod, Alan. Songs of the Wild West. 1991. illus. Simon & Schuster, $19.95 (0-671-74775-4).

Gr. 5–9. Forty-five songs, with musical arrangements by Dan Fox, are accompanied by intriguing background information and illustrations.

Blumberg, Rhoda. Full Steam Ahead: The Race to Build a Transcontinental Railroad. 1996. illus. National Geographic Society, $18.95 (0-7922-2715-8).

Gr. 6–12. Both celebratory and grim, this illustrated history conveys the excitement of technology and the terrible price paid by those displaced and exploited when the first transcontinental railroad shaped the West in the 1860s. Also by Blumberg, *The Great American Gold Rush* (1989) and *The Incredible Journey of Lewis and Clark* (1987).

Duncan, Dayton. People of the West. 1996. Little, Brown, $19.95 (0-316-19627-4); paper, $10.95 (0-316-19633-9).

Gr. 5 and up. With two other photo-essays, *The West* and *The Gold Rush*, this companion volume to the PBS documentary series is a fine introduction to the history of the West.

Freedman, Russell. Buffalo Hunt. 1988. Holiday, lib. ed., $19.95 (0-8234-1219-9).

Gr. 4–6. In this handsome book, Freedman describes how buffalo were worshiped and hunted to provide nearly everything the Plains Indians needed to stay alive—how the Indians' existence "found its rhythm in the comings and goings of the geat buffalo herds."

Freedman, Russell. The Life and Death of Crazy Horse. 1996. Holiday, $21.95 (0-8234-1219-9).

Gr. 6–12. A stirring biography of the

great leader of the Oglala Sioux. Among Freedman's other great titles are *Children of the Wild West* (1983) and *Cowboys of the Wild West* (1985).

Katz, William Loren. Black Women of the Old West. 1995. Simon & Schuster/ Atheneum, $18 (0-689-31944-4).

Gr. 6–9. Illustrated with impressive photographs and prints, this is an eye-opening account of the women who were activists, farmers, true pioneers, gold hunters, mail-order brides, black Indians, servants, and business owners in all areas of the West. Also by Katz, *Black People Who Made the Old West* (1977).

Marrin, Albert. Cowboys, Indians, and Gunfighters: The Story of the Cattle Kingdom. 1993. illus. Simon & Schuster/Atheneum, lib. ed., $22.95 (0-689-31774-3).

Gr. 6–10. Beginning with the introduction of horses and cattle to North America and debunking the romantic images, Marrin graphically chronicles the changes brought to the Great Plains as ranchers encroached on the area, particularly during the 1800s. Also by Marrin, *Black Indians: A Hidden Heritage* (1997) and *Empires Lost and Won: The Spanish Heritage in the Southwest* (1997).

Miller, Brandon Marie. Buffalo Gals: Women of the Old West. 1995. illus. Lerner, lib. ed., $14.96 (0-8225-1730-2); paper, $8.95 (0-8225-9772-1).

Gr. 4–7. With excerpts from journals and memoirs as well as photos from regional archives, Miller captures both the bone-wearying labor and the excitement that sometimes made living in the West worthwhile.

Ortiz, Simon J. The People Shall Continue. 1988. illus. Children's Book Press, lib. ed., $14.95 (0-89239-041-7); paper, $6.95 (0-89239-125-1).

Gr. 4–6. Simply told, this visual history of North America from the point of view of the American Indian shows the continuing struggle against cultural genocide since 1492.

Schlissel, Lillian. Black Frontiers: A History of African American Heroes in the Old West. 1995. illus. Simon & Schuster, lib. ed., $18 (0-689-80285-4).

Gr. 3–6. Schlissel focuses on black mountain men, homesteaders, soldiers, cowboys, and scouts, explaining their contributions to the taming of the frontier.

Turner, Ann. Grass Songs. Illus. by Barry Moser. 1993. Harcourt, o.p.

Gr. 7–12. In plain, lovely words, this collection of 17 poems tells of the journey west through the eyes of pioneer women. Also by Turner, *Mississippi Mud: Three Prairie Journals* (1997), in which three pioneer children describe their family's journey from Kentucky to Oregon.

Yue, Charlotte and **Yue, David.** 1986. illus. The Pueblo. Houghton, $14.95 (0-395-38350-1); paper, $6.95 (0-395-54961-2).

Gr. 6–8. With quiet authority, the Yues explore the origins and development of Pueblo Indian communities in the southwestern U.S., focusing on architecture and design rather than culture.

Fiction

Avi. The Barn. 1994. Orchard/Richard Jackson, $14.95 (0-531-06861-7); Avon, paper, $4.50 (0-380-72562-2).

Gr. 4–8. Set in the Oregon Territory during the 1850s, this is a classic survival story about kids who suddenly find themselves on their own without adults to care for them.

Byars, Betsy. The Golly Sisters Ride Again. Illus. by Sue Truesdell. 1994. HarperCollins, $14.95 (0-06-021563-1); paper, $3.95 (0-06-444207-1).

Gr. 1–3. An I Can Read Book, this is

the third collection of Old West yarns about May-May and Rose, with lively illustrations that capture the melodramatic posturing and comedy.

Conrad, Pam. Prairie Songs. 1985. HarperCollins, paper, $4.50 (0-06-440206-1).
Gr. 6–10. Young Louisa loves the solitude of the wide Nebraskan prairie, but Emmeline, the doctor's wife, can't adjust to the harsh pioneer life, especially to the loneliness.

Cushman, Karen. The Ballad of Lucy Whipple. Clarion, $15 (0-395-72806-1); HarperCollins, paper, $4.95 (0-06-440684-9).
Gr. 5–8. With zest and wit, Cushman gives us the domestic side of the western frontier adventure in Lucy's first-person story of how she hates being stuck out in the wilderness with her bossy, widowed mother.

Fleischman, Sid. Jim Ugly. Illus. by Jos. A. Smith. 1992. Greenwillow, $16 (0-688-10886-5); Dell/Yearling, paper, $4.50 (0-440-40803-2).
Gr. 4–6. Twelve-year-old Jake travels with Jim Ugly, his father's part-mongrel, part-wolf dog, trying to find out what happened to Jake's actor father in the wild world of the frontier West. Also by Fleischman are the wonderful McBroom tall tales.

Hudson, Jan. Sweetgrass. 1989. Putnam/Philomel, o.p.; Scholastic, paper $3.99 (0-590-43486-1).
Gr. 7–9. This is a moving, authentic story of a spirited young Blackfoot Indian girl who finds maturity thrust on her when hunger and smallpox decimate her tribe in the 1830s.

Lasky, Kathryn. Beyond the Divide. 1983. Simon & Schuster, $17 (0-02-751670-9); Aladdin, paper, $3.95 (0-689-80163-7).
Gr. 6–10. An Amish girl comes of age

and learns some hard lessons on the long wagon journey west to California.

MacLachlan, Patricia. Sarah, Plain and Tall. 1985. HarperCollins/Charlotte Zolotow, $14.95 (0-06-024101-2); paper, $4.95 (0-06-440205-3).
Gr. 3–5. Two children experience the apprehensions and joys of the possibility of a new mother when their father invites a mail-order bride to their prairie home.

Myers, Walter Dean. The Righteous Revenge of Artemis Bonner. 1992. HarperCollins, paper, $4.50 (0-06-440462-5).
Gr. 5–9. After Uncle Ugly is gunned down by that sneaky dog Catfish Grimes, who steals Uncle Ugly's treasure map, 15-year-old Artemis leaves his sainted Dear Mother and turns cowboy avenger in this madcap view of a wild Wild West.

O'Dell, Scott. Sing Down the Moon. 1970. Houghton, $16 (0-395-10919-1); Dell, paper, $4.50 (0-440-97975-7).
Gr. 6–10. Fifteen-year-old Bright Morning tells of the harsh journey of her Navajo people, who were forced to leave their homes as prisoners in 1864 on the long march to Fort Sumner.

Reaver, Chap. A Little Bit Dead. 1992. Delacorte, $15 (0-385-30801-9); Dell, paper, $3.99 (0-440-21910-8).
Gr. 9–12. Taught by his trapper father to do what is right, Reece doesn't hesitate to rescue a Yahi Indian boy about to be lynched by a couple of U.S. marshals, who later claim that Reece murdered a marshal, forcing the boy to find the Indian to prove his innocence.

Sherman, Eileen B. Independence Avenue. 1990. Jewish Publication Society, $14.95 (0-8276-0367-3).
Gr. 5–8. An engrossing story of a Jewish immigrant "greenhorn" who sails

from Russia to Galveston, Texas, in 1907 and then makes his way to Kansas City.

Yee, Paul. Tales from Gold Mountain: Stories of the Chinese in the New World. Illus. by Simon Ng. 1990. Simon & Schuster/Macmillan, o.p.

Gr. 6–9. Romance, loyalty, and justice are among the themes Yee probes in eight original stories based on the Chinese immigrant experience.

Yep, Laurence. Dragonwings. 1975. HarperCollins, lib. ed., $14.89 (0-06-026738-0); paper, $4.95 (0-06-440085-9).

Gr. 5–8. In this sensitive immigration novel, Moon Shadow leaves his mother in China and sails to America in 1903 to join his father, who lives in San Francisco's Chinatown, works in a laundry, and dares to dream of flying a biplane.

Artworks

by Stephanie Zvirin

Recently, there's been a virtual explosion of art books for young people, not simply books that help kids recognize fine art but also those that help them discover art in all that is around them. The following is a list of some of the best—for the classroom or just for pleasure.

Angelou, Maya. Life Doesn't Frighten Me. Illus. by Jean-Michel Basquiat. 1993. Stewart, Tabori & Chang; dist by Workman, $15.95 (1-55670-288-4).

Ages 4–8. In a picture book that shows how fine art can be used as illustration, bold abstracts capturing striking urban images are paired with a fine poem by a well-known writer.

Beneduce, Ann Keay. A Weekend with Winslow Homer. 1993. illus. Rizzoli, $19.95 (0-8478-1622-2).

Gr. 5–7. Written as though Homer is speaking to the reader during a friendly weekend visit, this nicely illustrated biography is one of the best in a stellar series.

Blizzard, Gladys. Come Look with Me: World of Play. 1993. illus. Thomasson-Grant, $13.95 (1-56566-031-5).

Ages 6–10. Questions prompt discussion of a group of diverse works, each of which shows children at play. Like others in Blizzard's artwork series, this is best used for lap sharing or with small groups.

Bolton, Linda. Hidden Pictures. 1993. illus. Dial, $14.99 (0-8037-1378-9).

Gr. 4–8. Van Eyck, Holbein, and Magritte included hidden, magical images in their paintings and drawings. Bolton shows us how to find them by using a mirrored sheet of paper that's included in the book.

Boulton, Alexander O. Frank Lloyd Wright, Architect: A Picture Biography. 1993. illus. Rizzoli, $24.95 (0-8478-1683-4).

Gr. 8–12. A handsomely designed, large-size book that uses photographs, drawings, and text to reveal both the personal and the creative side of the talented architect.

Children of Promise: African American Literature & Art for Young People. Ed. by Charles Sullivan. 1991. illus. Abrams, $24.95 (0-8109-3170-2).

Gr. 6–12. A combination of fine artworks and photographs with great African American literature reveals the image of African Americans, from slavery to modern times.

Davidson, Rosemary. Take a Look: An Introduction to the Experience of Art. 1994. illus. Viking, $18.99 (0-067-84478-0).

Gr. 5–8. A fine adjunct to the art curriculum, this introduces a variety of art-related topics—from the human form as a subject of art to art in religion and art as work.

dePaola, Tomie. Bonjour, Mr. Satie. 1991. illus. Putnam, $15.95 (0-399-21782-7).

Gr. 1–3. Artistic egos collide in a Paris salon when two rival painters, Pablo and Henri, both show up with their works. Older children may guess the artistic references; younger ones will simply enjoy the witty, colorful pictures and animal characters.

Florian, Douglas. A Painter. 1993. illus. Greenwillow, $14 (0-688-11872-0).

Ages 3–6. Dealing less with the creative process than with the technical aspects of art making, Florian conveys a word-and-picture portrait of an artist at work.

Greenberg, Jan and **Jordan, Sandra**. The Sculptor's Eye: Looking at Contempoary American Art. 1993. illus. Delacorte, $19.95 (0-385-30902-3).

Gr. 6–12. In a companion to their book, *The Painter's Eye* (1991), the authors marshal a striking assortment of examples to encourage kids to appreciate and express their own responses to sculpture. Also by Greenberg and Jordan, *The American Eye: Eleven Artists of the Twentieth Century* (1995).

Isaacson, Philip M. A Short Walk around the Pyramids & through the World of Art. 1993. illus. Knopf, $25 (0-679-81523-6).

Gr. 6–12. Isaacson explores how concrete elements such as color and form function in the abstract to help us see art in all that surrounds us, whether it be a quaint village in Nepal, an old fence in Quebec, or a grand painting in a famous museum.

Lehan, Daniel. This Is Not a Book about Dodos. 1992. illus. Dutton, o.p.

Ages 6–9. An outwardly simple story of a solitary artist whose existence is altered by the arrival of a flock of dodos demonstrates how experiences enrich and change our lives and inspire our art.

Macaulay, David. Black and White. 1990. illus. Houghton, $16.95 (0-395-52151-3).

Gr. 2–6. Telling four consecutive stories, each illustrated in a somewhat different but complementary style, this energetic picture book dares children to exercise their minds and eyes to discover common elements in the art and to simply have fun with the crazy combination of pictures. Macaulay is also the author/artist of several intriguing books that explore structures, among them, *Cathedral* (1973) and *Unbuilding* (1980).

MacClintock, Dorcas. Animals Observed: A Look at Animals in Art. 1993. illus. Scribner, $18.95 (0-684-19323-X).

Gr. 6–10. Known for her exceptional natural-history books, MacClintock celebrates animals in all their diversity and glory through a selection of 70 pieces by some of the world's great artists.

Mallat, Kathy and **McMillan, Bruce.** The Picture That Mom Drew. 1997. illus. Walker, $14.95 (0-8027-8617-0).

Gr. 2–4. In an instructive and joyful way to acquaint children with basic art terms and to introduce the idea of parts combining into a whole, Mallat's two daughters ostensibly explain how their mom goes about making a colored-pencil drawing.

McLanathan, Richard. Michelangelo. 1993. illus. Abrams, $22.95 (0-8109-3634-8).

Gr. 7–12. Part of the fine First Impressions series (others introduce Chagall, da Vinci, Cassatt, Wyeth, and several others), this is not only a lavishly illustrated volume but also a readable biography.

Micklethwait, Lucy. A Child's Book of Art: Great Pictures, First Words. 1993. illus. Dorling Kindersley, $16.95 (1-56458-203-5).

Ages 5–9. Expanding the idea she used in her I Spy books, Micklethwait organizes famous artworks by subject to introduce kids to what's in the world around them—boats, play, opposites, numbers, and much more. Micklethwait is also the author of *A Child's Book of Play in Art* (1996).

Micklethwait, Lucy. I Spy Two Eyes: Numbers in Art. 1993. illus. Greenwillow, $19 (0-688-12640-5).

Ages 5–7. Like its equally handsome companion, *I Spy: An Alphabet in Art* (1992), this uses famous paintings to present basic concepts and help children feel comfortable with two-dimensional art.

Moore, Reavis. Native Artists of North America. 1993. illus. John Muir, $14.95 (1-56261-105-4); paper, $9.95 (1-56261-231-X).

Gr. 2–5. Using the term *art* in its broadest sense, Moore introduces five contemporary Native American artists—two painters, a beadworker, a dancer, a musician, and a maker of dolls—in a colorful book containing photographs, comments from the artists, and projects that involve children in the art-making process.

Muhlberger, Richard. What Makes a Monet a Monet? 1993. illus. Viking/ Metropolitan Museum of Art, $11.99 (0-670-85200-7).

Gr. 6–12. Just one in an intelligent, well-illustrated series of art profiles that study the themes, composition, and techniques of famous artists by looking closely at some of their representative works.

Richardson, Joy. Inside the Museum: A Children's Guide to the Metropolitan Museum of Art. 1993. illus. Abrams, $12.95 (0-8109-2561-3).

Gr. 4 and up. Richardson conducts an armchair tour of the famous New York City museum, using lots of color photographs and intriguing facts about the many different things the museum contains. Another by Richardson is *Looking at Pictures: An Introduction to Art for Young People* (1997).

Rylant, Cynthia. The Dreamer. Illus. by Barry Moser. 1993. Scholastic/ Blue Sky, $14.95 (0-590-47341-7).

Ages 4–8. In a picture-book creation story, a solitary artist uses his scissors and paints to fashion the universe and everything that's in it.

Sills, Leslie. Visions: Stories about Women Artists. 1993. illus. Albert Whitman, $18.95 (0-8075-8491-6).

Gr. 5–8. A companion to *Inspirations* (1989), this profiles four women artists—Mary Cassatt, Mary Frank, Betye Saar, and Lorena Carrington—whose backgrounds differ as markedly as the work they've produced.

Talking with Artists. Ed. by Pat Cummings. 1992. illus. Simon & Schuster, $19.95 (0-689-80310-9).

Gr. 3–7. Although the 14 children's book illustrators in focus here may not be picture-lady material like Monet or van Gogh, kids know and love their work and will enjoy meeting them through these friendly "conversations." Cummings also edited *Talking with Artists, v.2* (1995).

Thomson, Peggy and **Moore, Barbara.** The Nine-Ton Cat: Behind the Scenes at an Art Museum. 1997. illus. Houghton, $21.95 (0-395-82655-1); paper, $14.95 (0-395-82683-7).

Gr. 4–9, older for browsing. This fascinating look at what goes on behind the scenes at the National Gallery in Washington, D.C., is as appealing to look at as it is informative as everything is explained from cleaning and repairing paintings to exhibit design, climate control, and visitor education.

Turner, Robyn Montana. Faith Ringgold. 1993. illus. Little, Brown, $16.95 (0-316-85652-5).

Gr. 2–6. Known for her "story quilts," vivid paintings, and Caldecott Honor Book *Tar Beach* (1991), African American Ringgold comes alive for young readers in a skillful entry in the Portraits of Women Artists for Children series.

Walker, Lou Ann. Roy Lichtenstein: The Artist at Work. 1994. illus. Lodestar, $15.99 (0-525-67435-7).

Gr. 4–6. Dynamite photographs, crystal clear, show one of America's preeminent pop artists at work in his studio.

Yenawine, Phillip. People. 1993. illus. Delacorte, $14.95 (0-385-30901-5).

Ages 5–9. A former director of education at New York City's Museum of Modern Art introduces art concepts and challenges kids to create imaginative stories based on what they see in famous pictures. Companion books deal with line, shape, story, and place.

Zhensun, Zheng and **Low, Alice**. A Young Painter: The Life and Painting of Wang Yani—China's Extraordinary Young Artist. 1991. illus. Scholastic, $17.95 (0-590-44906-0).

Gr. 4–8. This story of a Chinese child prodigy will attract children not only because of Yani's young age but also because the telling and the accompanying artwork are so gracefully presented.

Author Index

Haley, Gail E. 11
Hamilton, Virginia. 11, 15, 18
Harrah, Madge. 42
Harris, Jim. 3
Harvey, Brett. 48
Henkes, Kevin. 23
Herman, Charlotte. 39
Hermes, Patricia. 26
Herndon, Ernest. 18
Hildick, E. W. 31, 45
Hill, Kirkpatrick. 43
Hinton, S. E. 15
Hite, Sid. 7
Hoff, Syd. 26
Holland, Isabelle. 15
Horvath, Polly. 21
Howe, James. 29, 31
Hudson, Jan. 51
Hughes, Langston. 36
Hughes, Shirley. 26
Hurd, Thatcher. 30
Hurwitz, Johanna. 26
Isaacson, Philip M. 54
Jackson, Dave. 39
Jackson, Ellen. 3
Jacques, Brian. 7
James, Mary. 21
Jennings, Patrick. 21
Johnson, Angela. 26
Johnston, Tony. 26
Jordan, Sherryl. 45
Karas, G. Brian. 23
Katz, William Loren. 50
Keats, Ezra Jack. 15, 26
Keene, Carolyn. 15
Kehret, Peg. 18, 31, 43
Kellogg, Steven. 3, 11
Kerr, M. E. 39
Ketteman, Helen. 3
Kimmel, Eric. 39
Kindl, Patrice. 7
King-Smith, Dick. 7
Koller, Jackie French. 23
Komaiko, Leah. 26
Korman, Gordon. 21
Kroll, Virginia L. 39
Lamstein, Sarah Marwil. 39
Lasky, Kathryn. 51
Le Tord, Bijou. 40

Lear, Edward. 36
Lee, Jeanne M. 11
Lehan, Daniel. 54
Lehr, Norma. 18
L'Engle, Madeleine. 39
Lenksi, Lois. 15
Lester, Julius. 11
Levine, Gail Carson. 2
Levy, Constance. 36
Levy, Elizabeth. 30
Levy, Robert. 7
Lewin, Ted. 40
Lexau, Joan. 27
Lindbergh, Anne. 45
Livingston, Myra Cohn. 36
Lowell, Susan. 3
Lowry, Lois. 27
Lynch, Chris. 21
Lyon, George Ella. 46, 48
Macaulay, David. 15, 54
MacClintock, Dorcas. 54
MacGrory, Yvonne. 46
MacLachlan, Patricia. 51
Madhu Bazaz, Wangu. 40
Maguire, Gregory. 18, 23
Mahy, Margaret. 18, 43
Maifair, Linda Lee. 30, 40
Mallat, Kathy. 54
Mark, Jan. 40
Marrin, Albert. 50
Maruki, Toshi. 15
Mazer, Anne. 18
McDermott, Gerald. 11
McDonough, Yona Z. 40
McGraw, Eloise. 7
McKay, Hilary. 46
McKinley, Robin. 7
McLanathan, Richard. 54
McNaughton, Colin. 4
McPhail, David. 23
Meddaugh, Susan. 4, 23
Medearis, Angela. 31
Micklethwait, Lucy. 54, 55
Miller, Brandon Marie. 50
Minters, Frances. 4
Mitsumasa, Anno. 27
Moore, Reais. 55
Morpurgo, Michael. 40
Muhlberger, Ricahard. 55

Murphy, Elspeth Campbell. 30
Myers, Edward. 43
Myers, Walter Dean. 51
Namioka, Lensey. 27
Napoli, Donna J. 2, 43
Naylor, Phyllis Reynolds. 23, 30, 31, 43
Newman, Robert. 34
Nikola-Lisa, W. 4
Nix, Garth. 7
Oberman, Sheldon. 40
O'Dell, Scott. 51
O'Donnell, Elizabeth. 27
Ortiz, Simon J. 50
Osborne, Mary Pope. 31
Owen, Gareth. 18
Palatini, Margie. 23
Park, Barbara. 27
Parks, Ruth. 34
Pascal, Francine. 15
Paterson, Katherine. 11, 40, 43
Paulsen, Gary. 43
Pearce, Philippa. 34
Peck, Richard. 21, 46
Perrault, Charles. 12
Peterson, P. J. 43
Phillips, Ann. 18
Pierce, Tamora. 7
Pinkney, Andrea D. 48
Pinkwater, Daniel. 21
Prelutsky, Jack. 36
Pullman, Philip. 8, 34
Quackenbush, Robert. 32
Quindlen, Anna. 4
Raskin, Ellen. 32
Rathmann, Peggy. 24
Reaver, Chap. 51
Reiss, Kathryn. 46
Richardson, Joy. 55
Roberts, Willo Davis. 19, 32
Rogasky, Barbara. 40
Rogers, Fred. 27
Rose, Michael. 27
Rosen, Michael. 40
Roth, Susan L. 41
Roth, Susan. 30
Rounds, Glen. 48
Ruckman, Ivy. 19

Title Index